How To BREATHE WHILE SUFFOCATING

BRUCE W. BRACKETT

How To BREATHE WHILE SUFFOCATING

**A STORY OF
OVERCOMING ADDICTION,
RECOVERING FROM TRAUMA,
AND HEALING MY SOUL**

WILEY

Published by John Wiley & Sons, Inc., Hoboken, New Jersey.
Published simultaneously in Canada.

For general information on our other products and services or for technical support, please contact
our Customer Care Department within the United States at (800) 762-2974, outside the United
States at (317) 572-3993 or fax (317) 572-4002.

Wiley also publishes its books in a variety of electronic formats. Some content that appears in print
may not be available in electronic formats. For more information about Wiley products, visit our web
site at www.wiley.com.

Library of Congress Cataloging-in-Publication Data is Available:

ISBN 9781394217410 (Cloth)
ISBN 9781394217427 (ePub)
ISBN 9781394217434 (ePDF)

Cover Design: Paul Mccarthy
Cover Image: © Jenna Hokanson

SKY10067451_021624

I would like to dedicate this book to you, the reader, in whatever journey you are facing. To the person who is still struggling with their mental health. To those still facing active addictions. To the one who feels lost in the chaos and darkness. Also to the ones who have bravely recovered. I deeply want you to know that you are loved, and are not alone. Keep moving forward, for so much good is coming your way.

Contents

Preface

Have you ever felt like you don't fit the mold? Like an outsider who doesn't belong? Maybe you were bullied for being who you are. Perhaps you felt completely alone. If this sounds familiar, this book is for you.

Chances are that you or someone you know has been through addiction recovery. With eight billion people on the planet and a mind-boggling number afflicted, I can guarantee that you are not alone. This book is for you.

Has your life been shaken by trauma—physically, emotionally, spiritually? Mine has, and the reason I'm sharing my story is to connect with someone who needs it.

You will be meeting me in a very personal way over the coming chapters, so before we begin, let's be clear about who I am not. Though my name is Bruce Wayne Brackett, I am not Batman. I may share a touch of his notoriety (on social media, at least) and I aim to help people in distress. Unlike Batman, I do not have access to a thrilling array of gadgets to banish villains. That being said, we are all survivors. But unlike comic-book heroes, we face adversaries that are often hidden and hard to identify.

I am also not a supernatural being or some expert in human nature. I cannot explain why bad things happen or why evil exists, and I don't give advice on dealing with harmful people. But I offer hope. I have experienced the beauty of creation and I invite you to take a broader view to see that self-transformation is possible. When something insurmountable occurs, it is important to face it and to keep moving forward.

Finally, I am not Shakespeare. I don't have some deep insight into emotion, behavior, or the collective human condition. I don't try to explain why we do the things we do, or why we have contradictory beliefs, or where our opinions come from. But I can tell you that it is better to be than not to be. You are here. You are breathing. You have the opportunity to banish negativity and to invite positivity into your daily life. You can make the choice to keep moving forward.

■ ■ ■

So who am I? I was a child born with my fate already sealed. From the perspective of the medical staff who delivered me, it might have made more sense to inscribe my name on a tombstone along with a birth certificate. Given my circumstances, and by all outward assumptions, I was doomed to be a nameless statistic, a hopeless case, quickly discarded and forgotten.

Despite the odds being stacked against me from the very beginning, I continue to conquer all doubt. With each day, and through ever-unfolding challenges, I keep getting up, I keep finding the courage to stand tall—I keep moving forward.

I have had many failures along the way. I believe that failures can be celebrated because they prove that we are *successful at trying!*

As someone who has been affected by many traumatic events, I find a great responsibility lying at my feet. There were so many moments when I could have given up, but instead I overcame them. Whether you are trying to overcome, trying to transform, or simply trying to pass through your unique challenges, I hope the message of this book's title resonates with you. Breathe. Keep moving forward!

I offer my story as a source of hope and inspiration, and I tell it with a great passion for you. Whether you are held back by trauma, mental health challenges, or addiction diseases that affect you or your loved ones, you can overcome, transform, and pass through the experience. Simply put, if I was able to, so can you!

All details and stories that you are about to read are true from my own recollection and the memories about me from others who were present at the time. Some names have been changed in order to protect and respect those who chose not to be identified. Everything else is real.

This story is not pretty or easy, and certain passages might trigger some readers. This is a recounting of my personal experience. *Most importantly, this is not professional medical advice. If you are experiencing a mental health struggle, addiction, trauma-related issues, or a crisis or emergency, you should immediately reach out to a medical professional or emergency hotline. I have provided a listing of resources in the back of the book.*

Your situation is unique. I encourage you to read at your own pace and to find things we have in common. This way, you can connect to the elements that will resonate most with you.

Breathe . . .

Keep moving forward.

It's going to be okay.

1 | Born into It and Removed from It

Breathe. You can overcome the cards that you've been dealt.

Breathe. Just because some people let you down doesn't mean that all is lost. There are people who will be with you the entire way to love and support you.

Breathe. I know the weight of your situation might be unbearable without knowing the outcome of what is to be. That's okay; so much good is coming your way if you don't give up.

Breathe. Keep moving forward.

From the very beginning of my life, my mountains to climb were steep. As I was forming in the womb, I had already ingested drugs and alcohol, one of the many "crack babies," as they were known in the media at the time. I was born into a vast nameless social epidemic that was and continues to sweep the nation. Addiction and trauma don't affect just the people who suffer directly, but also the myriad of individuals and professionals who deal with the repercussions.

I was just moments old when I was rushed into detox from the addictive substances that I never chose to ingest. Days into my journey on this earth, I survived a double hernia operation. So not only was I born in the Rockies with literal mountains before me, but I also faced metaphorical mountains, large and looming from the outset.

Before we start walking in the weeds of my rough beginnings, let's begin with an actual mountain memory from my childhood, one that would come several years after those harrowing first years, one that is alight in happiness and fondness. I was perhaps seven or eight when Glenn, the man I would later come to call my dad, decided to take me and my sister for a hike up Old Baldy mountain outside of a cattle country hamlet known as Twin Bridges, Montana. It was close to 10,000 feet high, in my young mind high enough to touch the sun. That day was filled with fun, excitement, and a palette of new scents and sights: the color of the trees and hidden mountain vistas, the smell of newly emerging foliage and blooms. But even here, as in so much of my life, hid unseen, lurking dangers.

We laughed our way to perhaps halfway up the trail when we were surprised by an unexpected encounter. A grizzly revealed himself from behind a nondescript tree. He was at once terrifying and thrilling to see, and promptly dealt with by Glenn, who had faced such dangers before. He knew what to do to get us through and allow us to keep moving up the path. While we were paralyzed with fear, uncertain and overwhelmed, he assuredly turned, faced the looming grizzly, and made a New Year's celebration's worth of noise to scare it away.

What followed that brush with unexpected danger (and Glenn's courageous, protective, fatherly actions) was the reward of more joyful memories, more experiences to share. We kept moving forward, up the mountain. After the terror of the grizzly came a fragrant and gorgeous field of wildflowers and then a first for me: the exhilaration of reaching the summit of a mountain. From the summit, the view was majestic. I felt expansive and connected. The mountain no longer seemed impossible. The dangerous grizzlies, while still real and present, were not guaranteed to cause destruction, but were rather just part of this world around me. I could see them in the scale of what they were—big in the moment, but small in comparison to the larger journey, just one moment on the path.

At the top of Old Baldy, we found a pile of rocks where we could sit and rest. We were delighted to discover a forgotten glass jar that had taken up residence between several haphazard rocks. We freed the trapped jar, then wrote our names on scraps of paper and placed them within the jar before hiding it again under the rocks. Still the same jar, but now inscribed with our unique mark. It may still be there as a memento of our time at the mountaintop, or our names may have faded away, but we were there. We made it, and then we continued on.

Now, back to the metaphorical mountains of my early years. Being the only boy and having four older sisters, I would later discover that I was born into one of the worst reported cases of child abuse and neglect that the state of Montana had seen in the early 1990s. Beyond the trauma of that abuse, entering the world under the influence of drugs and alcohol would have a lingering presence that would affect every aspect of my experience for the rest of my life.

My earliest memory of my birth mother, Berna, is cloudy, much like the rings of smoke that perpetually surrounded her. I can remember being mesmerized by an orange glow that would rhythmically increase in intensity and brightness, then subside over and over again. She would breathe in and the tip of the stick in her mouth would grow brighter. She would breathe out and the intensity would retreat.

On, off. On, off. She lay in bed and smoke swirled upward. Her cigarettes are my earliest recollection, along with an internal sense of curiosity and haze.

Gillette, Wyoming. March 3, 1991. As usual in the '90s, the month of March was a typically brisk, almost burning type of winter cold. There was snow on the ground and the city of Gillette remained in its quiet hustle. Snow is present for most of the year in that part of the Rocky Mountains. I wonder, on the day I was born, how my biological mother, Berna, might have felt about having yet another child, her fifth. While most of my early memories are of her neglect, there were instances where she showed she cared, in her very Berna way.

There is a snowy day I have been told of, where she put me in the front basket of a snowmobile and drove me through the hills. My sisters and I were playing outside and I fell headfirst off a railing into a snowbank. My sister April yelled for Berna, who came running and found a comical sight, nothing but legs sticking out of the drift and flailing about wildly. She wasted no time pulling me out of the snowbank. We all laughed together.

The mothering instincts were there in some basic form, and so I allow her some grace. Had her own upbringing been different, perhaps she could have been a great caregiver and an invested parent. But that is not her, nor how my story goes. It is not even worth wishing for because it isn't the past that exists.

We bounced around a lot in that first year of my life, likely due in part to Berna's flakiness, but perhaps also to what I imagine was a possible sense of desperation. Though that area of the country was experiencing a drought at the time, I suspect Berna was drowning in a flood of forgotten towns and places, a rotating door of male figures, a variety of jobs, and a healthy dose of freeloading.

We landed in Sheridan, Montana, a quiet town of about 1,000 people. It is nestled in the majestic Rocky Mountains of southwest Montana in a gorgeous spot called Ruby Valley. The view holds its worth, its ruby treasure, which was not glittering red, but rather golden from the endless grass and hay that were present most of the year. Even though the earth was dry and dusty, the people who surrounded me were wet with liquor and the sweat of sexual encounters.

The Ruby Valley was overflowing with endless boredom and a stunning view of vast farmlands of wheat, corn, potatoes, and livestock. The treasure of the view contrasted with the ever-present smell of manure and, for my mother, infinite traps of drugs and alcohol.

Our small house was at the very entrance of the town, just off a main road. Despite the peeling paint, in my child's mind the house was massive and glorious. There was a decent-sized yard with trees and bushes, even a creek running alongside the property. The unkempt weeds and shrubs were part of the fun. I am told we played in the creek, unsupervised, quite a lot. Unlike the children of today's hawk-eyed parents, my sisters and I were not so much trusted as left to our own dealings, with an expectation that we wouldn't drown.

The house was dark, with dark wood paneling and furniture, and curtains that were always sealed closed. I suspect the curtain fabric had started off white but had turned a dull urine-yellow from the endless cigarette smoke. The cancerous haze was so thick that even the paint on the walls had started to absorb the putrid tint.

The entryway led into the living room, which had a furnace for heat. All of the furniture was ancient hand-me-down pieces, a mishmash of brown upholstery and forgettable prints. The kitchen was tucked in a small room toward the front of the house off the living room. The cabinets were usually empty and the refrigerator usually had something rotten in it. Most of the time, a foul smell would emanate from it, reminding us not to expect nourishment. On occasion, we had plain turkey sandwiches; other times we had nothing. Some days, my four sisters and I would share a single uncooked ramen packet.

Our home was filthy and disorganized, with garbage and clothes thrown in such a way that a tornado might have improved things. We did not have a pet, but the neighbors' dogs would welcome themselves in to poop, which would fossilize over time.

It is not my intention to describe Berna as a villain or a monster. She was a human, like each and every one of us. Had she been born into different circumstances or made different choices, life could have been different for all of us.

Berna was a physically beautiful woman with a tremendous smile and huge personality. She was personable, quick to make friends and easy to get along with when her mental health was good. She was talented and artistic. Had she not turned to drugs as a coping mechanism—a route of escape from her abusive father and own traumatic upbringing—she might well have even been a good mother. But she failed to break the cycle of abuse.

She stood about five-foot-seven and was a bit overweight in a way that accentuated her female form. Her hair was chestnut, long and wavy when dried and brushed out, curly when left wet. She was always cloaked in the suffocating smell of smoke, and her cracked lips were festooned with an endless parade of cigarettes.

My sisters are all older. April, the oldest, was around six when I was born, and she had dirty-blonde hair and a reserved, caring way about her. Sammi was five, with dark brown hair and an uncontrolled energy. Quiet, innocent Megan was three or four, with chestnut-brown hair, like Berna. Almost two, little Sonia was always getting into something, and she had dark, russet-red hair. Then I came into the picture, fresh little Bruce, almost always napping on the floor like an afterthought. At almost one year old, I was recovering from surgery, in a blanket on the floor. I am told that I was often left on the floor for nap time, even while I was also ill with chicken pox! A minor example in a larger pattern.

April, a small child herself, was the one really taking care of all of us. Not knowing much, but knowing that we were dirt poor, two of my sisters learned to steal bread and other odd food items from the local grocery store. We ate what we could, when we could. Malnourishment followed.

Berna didn't have the ability to adequately care for herself, let alone even one child. By the time she was in her mid-20s, she was a single mother to five young children, all with different fathers who were way out of the picture. Without the tools to cope, Berna became a very angry woman who turned to sex, drugs, and alcohol to deal with unresolved abuse and trauma from her own upbringing. The cycle had started to repeat.

Often, Berna would take a long, unannounced road trip with her friends, or go off with a boyfriend or even a complete stranger. She would abandon us at our grandparents' house for days, weeks, or months on end. We were once left for almost an entire year.

We mockingly called Berna's parents' house—our grandparents' home—the Pepto Pad, due to its markedly disturbing color. A trailer among trailers! Despite its creepily cheery exterior, the inside was entombed in even darker paneling than the house in Sheridan. By the time Berna was leaving us for long periods with them, my grandfather, who had abused her, had suffered a stroke. The experience had shaken him and he had changed his ways, so he didn't abuse us like he had Berna. As a consequence of the stroke, his speech was indecipherable, except on two occasions. During one of these, I managed to understand his garbling as "I love you." I said it back. Did I even know what that meant at that time?

My grandmother, a woman who clung fiercely to her religion, also said those words, but I was more interested in the copious supply of ice cream sandwiches she stashed in the freezer. She offered them to us regularly. I may have loved her back then. I definitely loved the ice cream sandwiches!

If Berna couldn't leave us with our grandparents, she would leave us with her friends or ex-boyfriends. That was almost never good. Once, while Berna was away, one of her "friends" agreed to "take care" of us. He locked one of my sisters inside a room with him. The situation was horrifying. We were terrified children, all under nine years old. One of my other sisters, desperately afraid, was brave enough to rattle the doorknob in hopes it would stop the man from his abuse.

The abuse would happen many times—to all of us.

When Berna happened to be home, she was oblivious, usually sleeping throughout the day because she was legitimately tired or simply hungover from the events of the night before. This left us unsupervised most of the time. We learned not to wake her unless it was truly an emergency. If we did, we got hit.

We would often be found by neighbors, naked, playing in the yard, in the creek, or frightfully, in the blind spot on the busy main road that passed just in front of the property line. On several occasions, strangers called the police reporting the naked children playing in the road. If Berna had to get involved, either because neighbors complained, the police stopped by, or one of us got hurt, Berna would beat us.

The beatings had a repetitiveness, if nothing else. Berna would usually beat the bare skin of our legs, backs, or bottoms with a familiar belt or stick. We also learned to watch out for a slap or good old-fashioned punch flying our way for unpredictable or inconsequential reasons.

One morning we were in the backyard during a rather nice and clear spring day. The dandelions that took over our yard were in full bloom, a sea of sunshine yellow. We meticulously picked through the abundance, selecting only the biggest, brightest, finest dandelions to create a gorgeous bouquet for our mother. We carefully took them inside, eager to surprise her. Our childhood intentions were pure and innocent. We simply wanted to give her something we thought was beautiful.

Berna threw them in the garbage, raging about how we had woken her up to give her weeds. She completely missed the meaning of that moment for us.

She always did.

Our relationship with Berna is a paradox. We were very scared of her, yet desperately hungry for her love and affection. We would cling to her in need, while cowering beneath her in fear, awaiting the back of her hand to meet our flesh if we complained of being hungry or because she accused us of being in the way or making a noise she found annoying.

When my sisters were old enough to attend school, they would primarily remain quiet and tend to themselves, when they managed to actually show up. My sisters definitely stood out amongst the other kids, but not for their achievements. Their hair was dirty and their skin was unclean. Their clothes and shoes were a battlefield of holes and they consistently smelled of urine. April acted as our surrogate mother. She made sure we had at least some clothing on, changed our diapers, and helped us with occasional baths.

April was doing all the parenting from the age of six onward.

Teachers at school noticed, almost immediately, that something was not right about our home life and started paying more attention.

After far too many reports of minor incidents with peers at school, not being potty trained, and numerous times being caught stealing food, school officials filed a report and a social worker got involved.

The physical evidence was impossible to ignore: bruises covering our bodies, constantly messing ourselves, and always, always being hungry.

Despite this, officials gave Berna a chance to change her ways. She was to sober up, keep a job, improve our living conditions, and stop abusing and neglecting us. But she simply lacked the desire to make any changes.

Some people claim my grandmother made the final call to social services, although she disputed this, perhaps to spare Berna's feelings, or in grief or shame or denial. That call brought the social workers and police officers to the door of our little Sheridan house.

It started as a typical day for us: not enough food but sharing what we had. One of my sisters, who had been playing outside, came running inside saying, "The lady is here. The lady is here."

When Berna saw the social worker with the police officers, she knew that was it. They took her outside, and when she came back in, tears streamed down her face.

Her emotions were on display: sadness, heartbreak, grief, despair. It may have been for us. It may have been for herself. I would like to think it was a combination of both. I had never seen her cry before, and I have never seen it since.

Berna and the social worker began to collect our most essential things, telling us to grab what we wanted. I had virtually no possessions of my own, but I remember vividly running around the house looking for my Batman slippers. I wore them all the time. They had significance because they were mine and because I was named after Batman. It was something I was connected to. I knew my life was about to change forever. I was about to be released from something I didn't even understand. I still hadn't found my Batman slippers—my connection to all I knew. I began to panic. *I need them!*

Then I was scooped up by the social worker, Terry. A police officer buckled me into a toddler car seat as Berna screamed for us.

It all happened very fast. One minute I was home, searching for my favorite Batman slippers, and the next I was in the back of a car without them. I can't remember taking a last look at Berna in that moment but I remember the car pulling out of the driveway and onto the highway.

I started to feel a very unusual sensation. I started feeling as if I were a balloon being pumped full of air. I was expanding, rising. I remember feeling tingly, like I was getting big all of a sudden. It was like I was growing and growing, to the point where my head might hit the ceiling of the car. I think it was the sensation of finally feeling safe and free. It made me feel bigger, feel the possibility of a new future.

It was still morning. My sisters and I sat quietly in the back seat. The social worker, Terry, was sitting in the front seat. I could see the back of her fiery red hair and skinny frame. After taking some silent deep breaths to herself she turned around in her seat to face my sisters and me.

"This is a very big day for all of you, I know. I am sure you have many questions and I want you to know that that is okay!" Her voice was firm yet tinged with an undercurrent of nervousness. "We are taking you children to stay on a beautiful ranch with lots of horses and cows for a little while," she continued.

After about 30 minutes that were thick with confusion and silence, the car arrived at a beautiful, sprawling ranch house in the heart of the Ruby Valley. The single-story home was a brick-red color. Its endless views of the Bitter Root Mountains were breathtaking. The view from our faded house on a busy corner had expanded to a grand and infinite view worthy of its crown in Big Sky Country. True peace and calm washed over me as the gentle breeze brushed through the blades of grass in the fields.

A woman, Sheila, and her husband, Bob, stood on their front porch awaiting our arrival as we drove up the long dirt driveway and pulled to the front of their home. Their arms opened wide welcoming us all as we slogged our way out of the car. I was not sure what was happening or why. All I knew was that we were free from Berna's angry, drunken rages. We were free from the abuse and starvation. Free from the unwanted sexual touch of her lovers and drinking buddies. We were free from the brutal beatings and pure neglect. We were free.

Breathe. I can overcome the cards that I've been dealt.

Breathe. Just because some people let me down, doesn't mean that all is lost. There are people who will be with me the entire way to love and support me.

Breathe. I know the weight of my situation might be unbearable without knowing the outcome of what is to be. That's okay, so much good is coming my way if I don't give up.

Breathe. I can and will move forward.

2 | The Foster Family

Breathe. No matter what it is that you are hungry for, you can find something that will satisfy your hunger, or someone to nourish you.

Breathe. Even in the chaos of the dust storms, when turmoil blows up in your face, remember that everything will settle back down, creating a sense of calm.

Breathe. Just because something may seem beautiful, shiny, and inviting does not mean it is for you. That's okay. If you keep going on your journey, you will find what is for you.

Breathe. Keep moving forward.

Sheila was a vibrant woman from Boston who had relocated to Montana with Bob, a sturdy Irishman who owned the ranch where we would be staying for now. For all I knew, that could be an hour or an eternity.

I know now that Sheila was a smoker. But unlike the ever-present carbon aura encasing Berna, Sheila was wrapped in the perpetual smell of mint to disguise her habit, always hidden just out of view of our impressionable young eyes. What was to be observed was her close-cropped dark hair and bouncing, bodacious energy. She kept her home immaculate, cleaning and vacuuming what seemed like four times a day. The gloss of freshly polished surfaces gleamed in the sunlight that drenched the interior through the grand picture windows.

Bob had a rare but hearty Irish humor that would crack through periodically, uncontained by his otherwise stoic demeanor. He fit the myth of the American rancher, always hard at work in the fields, never short of an extra chore to be tended. His very white Irish skin extended only to the edge of his shirt sleeves, where it was clearly divided at the border of a farmer's tan. He existed among horses and cattle in the sweeping fields that led to their home.

Entering this new world was a dream. I remember when we first walked in, Sheila asked us if we had eaten or were hungry. In fact, we were starving. *Malnourished* is the term professionals used during our first physical checkup after our removal from Berna's.

She quickly went to the fridge and pulled out food she had prepared for our arrival. All I can remember is heaps of mashed potatoes. I am sure there were other things like vegetables and probably slabs of turkey or chicken, but I remember the mashed potatoes. She heated them up and scooped a mountain-sized serving on each plate. "If you are still hungry, help yourselves to more," she said. *What!? Help ourselves to more?* Helping ourselves had *never* been an option before. For one of the first times in my life, I was properly fed, with actual, valuable nutrition.

My sisters and I were glued to the refrigerator, awestruck, in complete disbelief of the amount of food that was inside it. We had never seen so much food before. At some point, Sheila pulled us out of our mesmerized spell and away from the kitchen. It wasn't that she was worried about the copious amount of food we were sucking into our empty vessels, but simply that she was a very clean woman. Perhaps the mess of the feast was a bit too much for her on this first encounter.

After showing us to our rooms, she let us settle in and rest a bit. To be honest, I can't even remember the room. I was so overwhelmed by the chance to eat my fill that the room was of little consequence. I also started asking Sheila the two questions that I would come to ask over and over in the days that followed: "Where is my mommy?" and "Will you be my mommy?"

Later that first evening we had bath time. We were filthy. Even a moonless midnight could not have disguised that. But the grime covered a surprise. As the dirt slipped away, colors began to change. First the color of the water, from clear to coffee. But then our hair. To Sheila's amazement, she noticed that my oldest sister, April, had hair that was not in fact brown but a brilliant, almost translucent blonde. My sister Sonia's hair was not brown but a fiery red. The rest of our hair went from black to a beautiful chestnut brown.

We were truly clean for one of the first times in our lives. Looking back at it now, I am realizing that there were many firsts for us on this one life-changing day.

Over the course of the next few months, life at Bob and Sheila's was pretty typical. I remember the fields of golden grass swaying endlessly in the wind. Sometimes this same wind would kick up dust and create an amber-hued cloud that would whirl its way up the hills until its breaking point, whereupon it would fall back to earth. Bob would take us out on the horses as much as possible, whenever he wasn't tending to the daily life of the farm. While Bob was outside on the tractor or in the barn, Sheila would be inside cleaning every inch of the home. Between them, there was an unseen storm brewing, although we didn't realize it.

Rules were few with Sheila and Bob, save one important strictly enforced admonition. There was one very special room in the house that was entirely off-limits to us. It was shut off to the rest of the house by what seemed like cathedral-sized glass doors.

Through the panes we could see Sheila and Bob's precious, delicate curiosities, collected over a lifetime: glittering glass vases, fragile fine china, crystal-clear cabinets filled with ever more shining marvels and delicate figurines. The temptation could be resisted for only so long.

While both Bob and Sheila were out of the house on one otherwise typical day, temptation won. My sisters and I caved and pried open the silent, guarding doors. We hastily and silently snuck inside this glass chamber of treasures. Our awe was complete and utter. We had never seen such beauty before. Coming from a home with cigarette-stained walls and dog feces on the floor, imagine our delight to be in a home so clean, so spotless, with its very own room designated for crystal treasures!

We immediately investigated every cranny of this glittering cave of wonders, searching in astonishment, looking at every delicate detail of this marvelous menagerie of glass. This was my heaven! I am sure we were in its treasured walls for minutes, but it seemed like centuries.

Something caught my eye. Amidst all the breakable beauties sat something quite unlike the other items: a little pair of copper shoes. I didn't know what copper was at that time. I just remember being fascinated with them.

They were completely different from the shoes Sheila let me wear on afternoons when we would all play dress-up. Her red stilettos were irresistible to me. But at this moment it was copper that caught my imagination. Before I had finished marveling at this little metallic mystery, we heard the side door open from the garage and bulleted out of the room hoping not to be caught. Our only mistake: neglecting to shut the door behind us.

It must be stated that our punishment bore no resemblance to the type we had suffered at Berna's. After a light scolding for breaking the rule, as a punishment we were sent to bed early with no TV time.

The days turned into weeks, which quickly became months. Throughout, there were routine visits from the social workers assigned to our case. They updated us as to what the next steps were to be. Both Sheila and Bob wanted to adopt us very much, but their marriage was crumbling.

It was obvious to Sheila and Bob that we were too much to take on as they were working on their personal issues. One or both of them may have truly wanted to adopt us, but if we were to stay, we would surely break them apart. So, with a heavy heart, Sheila and Bob made the mature decision. It was time to have us move on to the next foster home. A lovely couple just a few miles away had heard of our case and was willing to take us on.

As the time of another transition neared, I became increasingly upset. Despite the millions of times I had asked her, I now understood, even as a very young boy, that Sheila was *not* going to be my mommy. This may have been the moment when I first started to learn and understand what my abandonment issues were. *Why won't she be my mommy? Where was my mommy? Who would be my mommy?*

Worried or not, I woke up one morning and it was time to move. Our belongings were again packed up, this time with care, into duffle bags and suitcases rather than carelessly thrust into trash bags.

The five of us piled into the social worker's vehicle and started our way along the dirt road that led down the valley hillside and across the Big Hole River. About 10 minutes later we entered a speck of a ranching town brimming over with all of 300 people. Twin Bridges was a place where everyone knew everything about everyone. There were more cows than people. The main street stretched a single mile long with a solitary flashing red traffic light that brought an unchanging rhythm to the center of town. We drove over a blue bridge past a giant silver water tower with a red-capped roof. Just beside the water tower and along the banks of the Beaverhead River stood a fairytale craftsman home with a vast fenced yard.

Out front on the porch stood a woman named Christine and her husband, Glenn. They were holding each other close as we pulled up in front of an iron gate, which had been painted a deep hunter green rather than a typical rust-laced black.

Christine was a truly beautiful women in her late 40s with shoulder-length brown hair. She was very lively and full of love. Her enveloping smile beamed from ear to ear as we arrived. Christine had retired as a flight attendant for Western Airlines. She was now working as a stay-at-home mother to her own biological son, Wade. I won't include memories of Wade other than to recall how much fun I had playing with him on the trampoline and how novel it was to have an older brother living with us, if even for a short time. Wade was nearly 18 years old when we came into the picture, so he was on his way out into adulthood in short order.

Glenn was a very handsome man blessed with movie-star looks. He was in his 50s with salt-and-pepper hair in a braid down to his shoulders. His presence was grand, in spite of a stature no taller than Christine's. Glenn's career had grown massive in this minor town, and he had a fabled reputation as a world-famous fisherman and fly-rod builder. His choice of career flowed perfectly with the rivers of Montana.

In single file we exited the car and stared in motionless disbelief at the property. We thought Sheila's and Bob's house was beautiful, which it was, but this house was huge, stunning, picturesque, and truly magical.

We passed through the gate and made our way to the front porch where, once again, two strangers reached out their arms to welcome us into their lives. After the social worker had introduced us all to each other, we remained awkward and quiet until Christine asked if she could pick me up. I nodded yes. Without missing a heartbeat she swooped me up and placed me on her hip, hugging me closely to her heart. *Will she be my mommy?*

"Let's go inside and show you all around. Come on, everyone," Christine boomed gleefully. She held me tight in her arms throughout the entire tour of our new home.

We had never seen such a house before. It had *so many rooms!* It seemed endless. To the left of the foyer was an office with stately built-in cabinets that perfectly framed a wood-burning fireplace. To the right was a sitting room with not one but two couches. Straight ahead was the living room with dark wood accents and another couch. *Three couches! They must be rich!*

Beyond the living room was a generous kitchen with an island and enormous windows that beautifully framed a view of the Beaverhead River. The tour continued as they showed us all the bedrooms. As we were standing at the top of the stairs on the landing, I remember looking up at Christine as she held me close to her heart and through my stammer I asked, "Will you be my mommy?"

Breathe. No matter what it is that I am hungry for, I can find something that will satisfy my hunger or someone to nourish me.

Breathe. Even in the chaos of the dust storms, I will find it blowing up in my face only later to have it settle back down, creating a sense of calm.

Breathe. Just because something may seem beautiful, shiny, and inviting does not mean it is for me. It could be a trap. It could belong to someone else . . . it is not always for me.

Breathe. I can and will move forward.

3

It Takes a Village, for Pain or Glory

Breathe. Sometimes you are in a situation that seems endless and hopeless. It's okay to ask for help. Sometimes it takes a village to give you the answers you are seeking.

Breathe. It may seem easier to give the answers we think others want to hear, but this is hurtful to our recovery. You must be honest with yourself to fully overcome and recover from challenges.

Breathe. Just because you have physically left your trauma behind does not mean it can no longer affect you. It follows you forever. The only way to fully recover is to honestly face it so you can deal with it and move on.

Breathe. Keep moving forward.

It took a few weeks to adjust to life at Christine and Glenn's. We were continually playing outside under the apple trees. As we settled into our new home and life, a cavalcade of curious people would come and go. Friends of the neighborhood brought copious dinners and a toy chest worth of gifts for us. Amongst the crowd of new faces, we recognized that one woman, Judy, came around far more often than the others. She was Christine's dearest friend and a former coworker at the airline. After her visits, her arms would be filled with clothes and books. Almost as frequently, Christine would go to Judy's house to get clothes and lipstick. This went on for several months. What started off small, some papers and cookware, developed into taking bigger things like chairs, pictures, larger pieces of furniture, and so on and so on.

We eventually realized that they had swapped houses. When Glenn and Christine first heard of our case, they knew instantly that they wanted to take us in. However, the house they were living in was a tiny two-bedroom with one even tinier bathroom. So Christine reached out to Judy with an astonishing appeal.

"Judy, we are taking in five foster children, and we don't have room in our home. Can we swap houses?"

"Of course!" Judy replied without skipping a beat. "It is basically just me in this huge house. Consider it yours."

And just like that we arrived, swept from the lives of Bob and Sheila and into the lives of Christine and Glenn and their many friends.

Almost as soon as we were introduced to the care of Glenn and Christine, we were also introduced to trauma therapy. Over the following months, we established a relationship with a therapist named Denise who lived and practiced in a town called Dillon, about 30 minutes away from little Twin Bridges. My sisters and I would ride in the back of Glenn and Christine's pristine white Dodge Caravan through the Ruby Valley, past the Beaverhead Rock, and across an endless sea of wheat dotted with thousands of grazing cows. This became our weekly routine.

I liked going to Denise's for one simple reason: she had heaps of toys in the waiting room and piles of children's picture books that I loved to look through. Christine read one particular book to me almost every time we were there. *Love You Forever* by Robert Munsch. There was a song in it that I loved to hear her sing to me. It spoke of a mother's unconditional love for her son.

I would ask her through my stammer to repeat it again and again. I needed to hear those words more than ever.

In that early time, and those first trauma therapy sessions, my memory doesn't seem to serve me well. I am sure I have blocked out certain experiences because it made it easier to move forward from that moment in time. It isn't my obligation to find meaning, nor offer forgiveness, although I may try and do those things. In my experience, the things I block out eventually make their way back to me, often not to the benefit of my well-being. My traumatic childhood shaped my early life, but the question remains: Will I create the mold that my life grows into? Or will I accept a future that has already been shattered by external forces? Making conscious choices in the direction of well-being allows me to move forward.

I remember spending countless hours in therapy simply playing with the toys, paying little attention to the questions that were being asked, typical ones like "How are you today?" or "Can you tell me what you remember that made you mad or upset?" I was four years old at this point and probably remembered considerably more than I do today. However, I was also avoiding talking about Berna's abuse.

I was just learning how to speak and wouldn't begin forming full sentences until I was five years old. My stammer left me unable to pronounce my Rs. I avoided speaking, and simply acceded to what I thought the therapist wanted to hear. If Denise asked me if I was sad, I would simply nod yes regardless of how I truly felt in that moment. This pattern of lying continued in and out of therapy.

One day in August, Glenn had a friend visiting. We called him Uncle Charlie, and he was a renowned photographer and visual artist. Charlie had made plans to head out to the Beaverhead River with Glenn to take some shots of him fishing. It was probably a last-minute idea to bring me along. When we arrived at a section of the river that was remarkably secluded and quiet, we began to gear up. Glenn put on his waders and Charlie assembled his camera. A serving of Smarties candies I had just devoured sent me running in circles and up and down the banks of the river. Another roll of Smarties was secreted in my camo pants.

"Hop on my shoulders, Bruce. Let's go fishin'!" he said, excited for any chance to enjoy his favorite pastime.

I dug into my pockets and reached out to him, clutching the candies in my tiny grip. "P-p-p-p-p-please," I stammered.

He opened the wrapper for me and then hopped down into the river, getting as close to the bank as he could. I walked over to the edge, grasping the candies in my hand. With one leg draped over his right shoulder, I swung the next leg over his left. He stood up fully, my meager weight a feather to his strength. He started to wade out farther toward the middle of the river, fishing rod in one hand with me tightly tucked on top of him. My head rested gently on his.

As we neared our desired spot, in a combination of excitement and comfort, I forgot the roll of sweets in my hand and let go. A rainbow waterfall of smarties cascaded from my fingers into the flow of the current and were quickly swept away.

I cried out, as if the treats had been stolen, rather than the casualty of a simple fumble. Ever the sturdy protector, Glenn didn't bother chasing after them. The current was too fast, and his priorities were with the precious cargo sitting on top of his shoulders. A huge pout consumed my face. I placed the side of my head on the top of Glenn's and looked back, glaring at Charlie, who was capturing the entire unfolding mishap on camera.

What could have been a completely forgettable moment in my childhood, became immortalized. Charlie had captured an iconic shot entitled "Dusk on the Beaverhead 1994," which has been mass produced into thousands of postcards and even ended up on the cover of a fly-fishing magazine in Japan.

Summer progressed to fall. We were adjusting to our new life, in our own ways and to the best of our abilities. Just because we were removed from the imminent trauma didn't mean that its presence was gone forever. It manifested in a multitude of ways: random outbursts of anger, constant lying, hiding our emotions. These were the forms of survival that we had relied on up to this point. They were familiar and ingrained. We were still afraid to express our real selves.

We continued attending the same church with Glenn and Christine that Sheila had had us attending during our time with her. Staying with this same congregation seemed the obvious choice as we were still adjusting to life with our new foster parents.

Notre Dame Church was a little white church with a steeple that rose above the surrounding treetops. Halfway through each service, the younger children were either paraded into Sunday School or released outside to play, supervised, while the church services continued.

Our routine at that point in the service, however, was to head across the street with a family that had babysat us many times.

This family was very well known within the ranching community. Often, the mother wouldn't stay, leaving her son to watch us alone, much like the many times Berna left us alone with random men.

What I remember is being in his bedroom with the door closed and probably locked. It usually was. I was playing video games, sitting on his lap. I also remember becoming petrified, unable to move as he began playing with me, down there. This abuse, once again, became part of our routine.

One day, I remember sitting on his lap and being fondled, and then the next thing I remember is being on our porch at home with Christine guarding me, police officers by her side. One of my sisters, thankfully, had the courage to squeal on him.

Unlike me, Glenn and Christine remember the conversation with the police like it was yesterday. "Unfortunately, we are not surprised by this coming from that family," they reported. "We have dealt with this before." Glenn and Christine were completely heartbroken. Discovering even more abuse, happening under their watch, crushed them. We never went to Notre Dame Church again.

Church of the Valley was the next option for us. Like Notre Dame, it was a little white church with a steeple rising to the sky, just on the opposite side of our tiny town. This was a Methodist Church whose members included longtime friends of Glenn and Christine. Glenn sang in the choir every Sunday.

My age meant that I went to the church's day care (no more offsite babysitters for us), which I loved! When the weather was nice, we could run around and play outside in the fenced-in safety of the back-yard. An elderly man would pass by on his walks. He would hobble up to the fence and delight us with butterscotch candies. His care and good nature were genuine. As wintertime weather descended, we would play in the church's recreational room, which was by far my preferred place to play. In the corner, a trunk concealed a bounty of joy: dress-up clothes and dresses! The bigger the sparkle, the bigger the desire! I would twirl carefree in a whirl of fabrics that fanned out as I spun in innocent ecstasy. Playing Barbies with the girls was another of my delights. But it was only a short year before a new pastor arrived and changed too many of the traditions at Church of the Valley, and so my family and many others stopped attending.

On one of our last days of attending Church of the Valley, we were walking back home after the service. It was just two short blocks away. Before we made it back to the house, we encountered a section of freshly poured concrete. The sidewalk was just beginning the process of curing. Glenn got the silly idea to have me place my hands in it, so that I could leave my mark. I sat down on the ground as he crouched down around me, helping to hold my hands still and pressing them down into the wet pavement. We waited a few moments before pulling my hands back, revealing two tiny handprints. Glenn pulled out his red Swiss Army knife, a tool that he always carried, and scratched "Bruce 1995" in the new pavement.

In therapy, Denise continued to work with me on my ongoing question: Will you be my mommy? "Christine is your mommy, Bruce," Denise would reassure me. It took time, but when I finally started to trust things more, I started to call Christine and Glenn, "Mom" and "Dad".

One of my sisters, who was eight years old at the time, had a different story. One night we had a family meeting while sitting at the dinner table in the kitchen. It was dark, and we could hear the sound of the river outside. It was high and rushing by, carrying away any helpless fallen leaf that landed in its current. Mom and Dad began to explain their concerns about being able to give her the care she needed, as well as their love and hopes for all of us. So much hard work and good fortune had allowed us to stay together to that point, but my sister would not continue living with us. I wept as I thought of her being swept out of our lives. To me, it felt like the death of my sibling.

As I got older, I had a hard time fitting in. Even at doctors' appointments, people passed judgments on me. I was not yet the author of my life.

"We believe that Bruce has a gender disorder," one doctor would say.

"How can you say that? He is only five. He doesn't have a gender disorder. He is gay," my mother would retort boldly.

"Well, he is so young, I don't know if you can say that yet about him," the doctor would reply.

"Exactly, so you can't say that he has a gender disorder," Mom would further respond, the Cheshire Cat smirk on her face announcing her reasoning-victory, as she proved their argument wrong.

Time strode on. I began first grade. This is when many things would change for me. I had just overcome my stammer and was speaking much more clearly. I was starting to catch up to the other children my age. But I still couldn't pronounce my Rs correctly and would use a W sound instead, so "My name is Bruce," would come out as "My name is Bwooce." Kids being kids, the bullying began. Not only did they make fun of me for my speech, but they picked on me relentlessly because I was more flamboyant than the other boys.

One day I was sitting at my desk, doing my schoolwork, when a woman knocked on the classroom door. I hadn't even looked up from my paper when my stomach turned with an unsettling feeling because I could sense that she was there for me. After briefly speaking with the teacher, the mystery woman started walking in my direction.

My eyes locked on my paperwork in futile defense. She squatted down next to my desk and said, "Hi, Bruce. My name is Vivian. I am a speech therapist here at the school. I was wondering if we could take some time to talk." In spite of my dread, through my peripheral vision, I managed to see a gentle smile warming her face.

"Am I in t–t–twouble?" I ventured, my gaze still locked on the paper before me.

"My goodness, no! I just want to take some time and hang out with you and get to know you a little better. Can you put your work in your desk and come with me?" She reached out her hand. I did as she said and grabbed her hand as we walked out the classroom door and up the hallway into the high school section of the school building, where Vivian had an office.

For three years, I visited her office two times a week to work on my speech. I absolutely hated it because facing my speech impediment made me feel stupid.

During these years with her, the bullying continued unabated. One day my third-grade class was getting ready for breaktime. Our teacher had a clawfoot tub in the corner filled with pillows. If you had earned enough stickers for good behavior, you could pick a book to read while you enjoyed sitting in the tub. That day, the teacher invited me to be the bathtub reader. As I got up and grabbed a book, one of the bullies snapped, "Where do you think you're going?"

"I am going to *read* in the tub," I smartly replied. Then I noticed what had just happened. I had said the R correctly.

It hadn't escaped the bully's attention either. "Whoa, wait, say that again," he said, taken slightly aback.

"I am going to *rrread*, in the tub." I announced slowly and emphatically.

The bully was overcome with both surprise and disappointment. "Aw, man! Now I'll have to find something else to make fun of you for," he remarked. I rolled my eyes and kept walking to my reward, feeling awash in pride.

My relief after I graduated out of speech therapy was short-lived. These sessions were followed with enrollment in special education classes. Even with my improvements in language, I was still falling behind in every subject except for art class. That was my favorite.

When fall came, my sisters and I would play in the leaves. When winter came, we would make snowmen or dig tunnels in the fresh powder, pretending to be little fairy creatures living outdoors in nature. We would jump on our trampoline, temporarily shrouded by a wall of white, as the snow bounced upward and we plopped down. At home, sheltered from the closed-minded public ever present about town, life was pretty good. We were given everything we needed and most things we asked for.

My parents, seeing that we enjoyed art and possessed a natural talent for it, decided to turn the dining room into an arts and crafts room. They completely transformed the dining table into an arts workshop, with every imaginable art medium: acrylics, pastels, markers, crayons, pencils, glitter, molding putty—the list went on and on. What might have simply felt like play to us was also a spontaneous and unfiltered therapeutic release. My mom would save the best creations from each of us and later enter them into the Twin Bridges Art Fair, which took place every summer at the fairgrounds. Almost without fail, we would each come home with ribbons of success. This gave me great joy and pride. *Finally, something I was actually good at!*

As I mentioned earlier, Glenn and Christine gave us everything they possibly could. We would take an entire month each summer to go on a vacation. Our big family would live together in a pop-up camper as we headed farther west to visit our parents' friends in

Seattle and more family and friends in Northern California. Both Glenn and Christine were originally from the Bay Area, so a lot of their family and friends were still there. Glenn's parents, Meme and Pop, lived in Walnut Creek, and Christine's brother Bob and his husband, Jack, lived in Vallejo just off the Bay. This was, without question, my favorite time of year. I loved going to see them.

Meme and Pop had a true sense of humor and would spoil us rotten. One day Meme asked if we wanted some ice cream. We all nodded our heads, happy and eager. She came back with a miniscule scoop of vanilla ice cream. A single teaspoonful, at best, for each of us. Imagine our disappointment. To further the gag, she would promise to go back and get us toppings, only to return and offer us some raisins. We didn't want to be rude so, trying to disguise our obvious frowns, we would accept. "Sure, I will have just a little bit." Then she would return with a colossal bowl, overflowing with raisins. This confused us but made us laugh.

Christine's brother Bob was just the same, warm and funny. Spending time with him was eye-opening for me. It was rare for a kid of that time to be able to see two men living their truths authentically as husbands. They were in love and openly gay. That open acceptance was a contrast to the darkness and denial that existed in Montana, and it would make a lasting impression on me. Bob's husband, Jack, was also an artist and he would send us Halloween costumes that he had made. I remember two, vividly. One was a glittery purple dragon and the other a blue jester with a long flowing cape.

I would have loved for these vacations to continue forever, but as we grew up and took on more responsibilities, traveling in the summer became harder to accommodate. Our visits to the extended family became less frequent with the passing years and eventually stopped when I was 10.

■ ■ ■

I was now six years old. As we got older, the hot topic of our adoption became more and more regular at home and in therapy. Glenn and Christine were intent on adopting us, and we were willing. This became a huge relief for me as I knew I had finally found my mommy and daddy. Although it remained a lingering fear of mine, I understood that I wouldn't lose them, and more importantly, I felt certain that they wouldn't abandon me.

November of 1997 came around. Our adoption date was finalized, and we were on our way to the capitol, Helena, Montana, for the adoption ceremony. This would be the first of Montana's adoption ceremonies hosted by Governor Marc Racicot. The adoption ceremony had been designed so that many selected families could follow through with the adoption process all at once. I remember Glenn parking the car and we all hopped out, dressed in our best. The leaves had already turned and fallen to the ground. On our way to the capitol's rotunda, we shuffled through them along the sidewalk, kicking up little flurries of color.

The capitol building was a huge structure with a massive dome. As we entered, the rotunda echoed with a cacophony of footsteps, talking, and laughter. There were 15 to 20 other families there. The ceremony began with a rotating podium of legal professionals, introductions, and speeches. Then the governor took his place at the podium. One by one, in succession, each family approached the podium to be sworn in under oath. A slew of questions were asked, with the participants each responding yes, acknowledging the adoption process.

Then it was our turn. We were instantly out of the tedium and into the meaningful. Our improbable crew were about to be linked in perpetuity. We walked up to the podium, stood next to the governor, and were sworn in under oath. I don't remember a word he said. I just remember leaning up against my new mom and holding her hands tightly as they were draped over my shoulders. Each of us raised a hand and agreed to the terms and understanding of the adoption.

In as little time as it had taken to assemble our troupe into line, our lives were changed forever. We were officially adopted by Glenn and Christine. For the first time in our lives, we had a say in our future. I was on a path forward because of the security that came with the adoption. We were officially a family.

The entire process of getting up to this point had taken five different therapists, an avalanche of paperwork and social service meetings, and almost the entire village of Twin Bridges to help ensure this possibility came to be. Finally, we were truly home.

Breathe. Sometimes I am in a situation that seems endless and hopeless. It's okay to ask for help. Sometimes it takes a village to give me what I am seeking.

Breathe. It may seem easier to give the answers I think others want to hear, but this is hurtful to my recovery. I must be honest with myself in order to fully overcome and recover from challenges.

Breathe. Just because I have left my trauma behind does not mean it can no longer affect me. It follows me forever. The only way to fully recover is to honestly face it so that I can deal with it and move on.

Breathe. I can and will move forward.

4

Bullies Be Gone!

Breathe. Not everything is *for you* to understand.

Breathe. What others say or think about you is none of your concern.

Breathe. You may not have control over what is said or done to you. However, you do have control over how you handle this information or situation.

Breathe. Keep moving forward.

Let's just say that first grade through fifth grade was no cakewalk for me. Being with the same kids year after year meant being bullied and teased for the same things year after year. I absolutely hated school. The only relief was a handful of friends—Addy, Rachel, Kylie, and Jessica—our bonds made in our shared status as outcasts. Strangely, I had a few other friends who would waffle between wanting to play during the summers and bullying me during the school year. This odd ritual existed as a result of their own experience being bullied. Our friendship was valued out of view, but a liability in sight of schoolmates.

Despite many meetings with my parents, the teachers, and the principal about what to do about the bullying, I was suffering. To this day, I still don't fully understand why the teachers and administrators never disciplined the bullies. When the teachers did catch someone bullying me they would simply call them out and say, "That's enough." Occasionally a few times the bully *and* I would be sent to the principal's office for disturbing the class.

One day at recess, one of the kids who befriended me in summers and bullied me during the year saw me playing on the slide. I had made a series of rapturous loops, bolting up the steps, barely stopping at the top before gliding gleefully down. On one such loop, he was waiting for me at the bottom.

"Hey Bruce, I hear you are a queer. You know what that means? You are a sissy," he taunted. I didn't actually know what *queer* meant. I tried to ignore him as I hopped off the slide and made my way back to the ladder. As my foot raised to take the first step, he stopped me. "Didn't you hear me, faggot? You're a sissy queer!" His voice becoming louder and more assertive.

"Leave me alone, Zach!" I blurted out. Then he pushed me. Hard. I fell backward, scrapping my elbow on the dirt. Scenes like this were an almost daily occurrence. But this time was different. I jumped up so fast Zach turned and ran in the opposite direction. Propelled by years of the pent-up rage, I started to chase him.

"I'll show you! Call me quee-aw one more time," I shouted, pissed at myself for mispronouncing my R.

Through nervous laughter, he shouted out to his buddies, a feeble attempt at masking his embarrassment that our interaction wasn't the easy, certain victory he had anticipated. "The queer still can't pronounce his Rs."

Like an angry bull facing the taunts of a matador's silken cape, I ran after him in full force, this time ready to kill. I only remember seeing and hearing red. "I'm going to bite your balls off! I'll teach you," I screamed and repeated, "I'm going to bite your balls off!"

Out of nowhere, my face burned as his punch landed squarely on my cheek. I stumbled back, regained my balance, and punched back. We exchanged blows in equal measure for the length of a child's forever. Two teachers on recess duty came running in our direction and pulled us apart. "*That's enough!* Both of you, to the principal's office. *Now!*" shouted one of the two.

We both sat in silence in the principal's empty office. We shared a desire to avoid interacting with the other and a worry over our mutual fate. The ignorance of time during our brawl had transformed into a menacing clicking of the clock. When the principle finally entered, he offered not a word to us. He sat down, picked up the phone, and called both of our parents to inform them of what had just happened.

An hour passed. We were still imprisoned in our chairs, motionless, silent, and forced to sit on our hands. The end of the day finally arrived, along with our parents. Under their respective gazes we were forced to apologize to each other, the shared resentment and insincerity obvious.

The look on our parents' faces revealed that a difference in fate awaited. I could tell when Zach's father picked him up that he was in big trouble. I didn't know this at the time, but bullies typically learn their cruel behavior at home. I can only imagine what he had coming to him that night.

My fate, on the other hand, was surprisingly cool. Instead of punishment, dad took me to the Shack, a local pizza and ice cream shop just down the street from the school. I was rewarded with a heaping bowl of ice cream for finally sticking up for myself.

The relief was short-lived. Each year, the bullying got worse. Nasty notes were written about me and shared throughout the class. At recess or in the hallways, I was pushed around. One day, while leaning over the fountain to get a sip of water, a boy came up from behind and dropped his backpack full of books on my head. My teeth hit the waterspout, chipping my front tooth. Getting bullied stinks. Literally. Some junior-high kids once tossed an open Ziplock bag of pee at me yelling, "Think fast! Catch!" Their behavior was as disgusting as I felt while soaked in the offender's urine. While I grew in stature, the list of assaults, both verbal and physical, grew as well.

It came to a climax in sixth grade. We had been assigned to do an inspirational report on any topic we chose. When we finished, we were to read them in front of the class. The first topic that came to my mind was to do a report honoring my uncles in San Francisco. It would tell of how they inspired me to be honest about who I am. Every word shared a bit of my truth about how Uncle Bob and Jack were role models, two amazing professionals succeeding in life. It told of how proud I was to have them show me that it was okay to be me. I was proud of this report and the hard work and honesty that I had put into it.

The due date came for all of us to read our reports in front of the class. For reasons I do not remember, I was not in school on the day we were to read the reports aloud. I never got a grade on the report, and I never received it back.

It wasn't until much later in life that I found out what had happened that day, courtesy of my fellow band of honest outcast friends. The teacher had decided to use my report as an opportunity to preach to the rest of my classmates. I am told that he ceremoniously walked my report to the front of the class and plopped a trash can down forcefully to create a loud sound that echoed his contempt.

"This report is not worth reading out loud. I just wanted you to know that it is about two homosexual uncles, and this type of garbage will *not* be tolerated in my classroom! This is wrong, this is sinful, and an abomination. Bruce's uncles, and Bruce too, if he follows their ways, will go to Hell!" He angrily spat on the report and then chucked it into the waste bin.

I doubt it was his intention to "save" me, but, ironically, in a way he did. He saved me from having to come out of the closet as gay at school. He took that liberty himself. The fallout was immediate. When I returned to school, I was subjected to a nonstop loop of "Bruce is a sissy", "Queer", "Faggot", "You can't be in the locker room because you are going to look at us."

I was forced to change for PE in a separate bathroom. In some regard, that was a relief. I didn't mind being separated because I was afraid of most of the boys anyway.

Coming out to my family, however, was an entirely different story. I remember one night, after skiing at Discovery Mountain, I sat my parents down on the couch in the living room. In an action that seems cute in retrospect, I patted the couch next to me, as I sat in the middle, encouraging my parents to sit on either side of me. "I have something to tell you both," I said nervously. My parents sat down willingly and probably already knew what was coming. I continued, "While we were skiing today, I noticed that I was watching all the snowboarders. I like snowboarders. They are cool."

I fumbled trying to figure out exactly how to say what I was about to reveal. "I mean like, I was *watching* them. I was getting excited if you know what I mean . . . I . . . I think . . . I'm gay." I finally blurted out. Not a second went by before my mom grabbed me in her arms and my dad put his hand on my head.

"Oh, Bruce, we know . . . and we love you," they both said, almost laughing.

Our school in Twin Bridges was very small, maybe 150 kids from preschool through 12th grade. Each year, the school held a spring fling party to which the entire town was invited. We would all pile into the high school gymnasium, transformed through the simple addition of snacks, soft drinks, live music, and lots of dancing.

This was a chance to let loose. And boy, did I. I remember dancing in the middle of the floor, loving every minute until I started to get shoved around by the usual bullies. That night, it was too much. I went home sobbing. I would never fit in. I ran into the house and into my mother's arms, telling her everything that had just happened. Apparently, she had had enough, too. We spent the remainder of the evening practicing how to confront bullies.

Unbeknownst to me, she had been doing research. She had gone online and printed out a worksheet. We practiced step by step. First, we did some role playing. She pretended to be a bully and shoved me around the living room, teaching me how to stand up for myself. Using one of the examples she shouted, "Your mother lives in a dumpster."

I was to reply with, "Yes, she does, and boy, you should see it. It's pretty nice. Nice and smelly."

She followed up with the next example. "I bet you sleep in the dumpster with her."

I was then to reply, "Yes, I do. I actually just got some new pillows too that I think will spruce up the place. Want to come over after school and help me decorate it with her?"

One of my mom's favorite comebacks in response to the bullies was, "Were you dropped on your head?" She was teaching me to stop reacting with defense or anger and to start going along with the taunts. The more I went along with insults, the less fun it would be for them to bully me. Then, hopefully, they would get bored of me and move on.

I took this advice to school and put it into practice. Within two months of using these new techniques, like magic, the bullying slowed down to an almost nonexistent level. Of course, I was still subjected to the random one-offs, but I didn't give in.

Eventually school became an *almost* livable and breathable place. I felt slightly freer to be myself while there. In sixth grade I came out as gay to my true friends: Addy, Rachel, Kylie, and Jessica. Children are more perceptive than they are given credit for. They all knew it already and welcomed me with open arms. They also promised to keep it a secret. Their loyalty and promise of secrecy was welcome, but wasn't necessary. Everyone else already knew too.

Once I started living my truth without caring about what others had to say, my bullies no longer had ammunition to bully me with. I no longer reacted to them in the way they wanted me to. They wanted me to be hurt and cry. When I stopped doing this, and either agreed with them or even just fully ignored them, they gave in and gave up. I am sure they found their next target. But I had become too busy to notice because the next chapter of my life was already unfolding.

Breathe. Not everything is *for me* to understand.

Breathe. What others say or think about me is not of my concern.

Breathe. I may not have control over what is said or done to me. However, I do have control over how I handle this information or situation.

Breathe. I can and will move forward.

5 | Am I a Star? Meh, Same Difference

Breathe. You are capable of being yourself and stepping into your light, despite how difficult it may be. You are capable.

Breathe. With great success comes the temptation to ruin it, but you don't have to.

Breathe. We are all the same in many different ways. We truly share the "same difference."

Breathe. Keep moving forward.

When I was in fifth grade my mom had me audition for a local theater company called the Missoula Children's Theatre. Landing my first role as Sing Sing Sam in the light musical *Treasure Island* also landed me a new home: the theatre!

In sixth grade, I auditioned for more shows at the Orphan Girl Children's Theatre, a community theatre group in Butte, Montana. The energy and excitement of the touring Broadway shows that danced on the stages of the Mother Lode Theatre—just above our modest 100-seat space in the basement below—trickled down into the imaginations of our little troupe and we dreamed of joining those grand tours. My first production in its humble basement walls was *The Emperor's New Clothes*.

This was the first time I found friends outside of Twin Bridges. The theatre director was gay and a few of the other children were too. I had finally found my people. It wasn't long before the kids of the Orphan Girl got to taste the elixir of performing upstairs at the Mother Lode. We were entranced by the series of arched golden lattice that formed the proscenium above its massive stage. Swags of velvet and tasseled fringe lifted our dreams skyward as we peered at the grand main curtain high above. Twelve hundred glorious red seats begged for the audiences that would cheer our names and applaud our efforts. I began to thrive in my new surroundings. The upcoming production was to be *Oliver!*, an adaptation of the Charles Dickens novel *Oliver Twist*. Its story of a starving orphan boy, about my age, was too similar to ignore.

In this same period, my mom was working as the store manager for a candy shop in Virginia City that her best friend, Judy, owned. I wasn't of the age to legally work yet but I was happy to help out in this candy paradise, which was like something out of the movies. Virginia City is either a faithfully preserved historic site or a visually appealing tourist trap. Summer sees a rush of visitors echoing its original lustrous draw, the Gold Rush of the 1800s.

Like many summer towns known for swelling with tourist dollars during the pleasant weather months, Virginia City has not one but two professional theatres. Auditions for *Oliver!* were fast approaching, so my mom drove me to Virginia City to solicit some expert advice. We met with the director of the repertory theatre company, famously known as the Virginia City Players, who perform at the Virginia City Opera House. This temporary mentor passed on valuable information, and I soaked it up. He coached me on how to succeed at auditioning. We worked on my song choice, "Lean on Me," and a monologue about a boy wanting an ice cream sundae. Given how much I could relate to that topic, the acting took care of itself!

Audition day arrived. I felt confident: a true professional was coaching me!

My clothes looked the part, and I was sure my 16 bars would be a home run. The process would be standard for the musical theatre: first we would sing, then present our monologues, and finally dance. Each part of the unfolding process felt easier than the last. The difficult part would be the waiting. The results of the audition would be posted online, so we were told to check regularly for updates.

My mom and sisters were working in Virginia City, busy with the end-of-season tasks to close the Wonka-worthy candy shop. I was stuck back in Dad's workshop, with the sticky task of cleaning up wood glue for the bamboo fly rods that had taken up residence on the cement floor. I dutifully finished my task, and Dad released me for the day. With my belongings gathered, I began the walk home. "Be sure to check the computer for the audition updates," he called out as I walked across the street. I bolted across town toward my computer-screen finish line.

Logging in and waiting for the dial-up to finish connecting to the internet was the '90s version of teenage torture. It seemed to take forever because it *did* take forever. Once I finally connected, my fingers could barely type the website the theatre director had given us to check the results. If I could have looked at myself in this moment,

I would have surely been blue, about to pass out from nerves and holding my breath.

I scanned the lines of names and roles. *Where, where, where was mine?* My eyes landed on it: *Oliver Twist . . . Bruce Brackett.* I froze. *No possible way!* I was overwhelmed, which led to uncontrollable sobbing. I spun around in the swivel desk chair, making several rotations before I managed to reach for the phone.

"Cousin's Candy, how can I help . . . " my mom began before my breathless shouts cut her off.

"*I got it! I got the part!*" I screamed into the phone.

"What?! Which part?" her voice anxiously probed.

"*Oliver, I got the role of Oliver!*" I was still screaming and crying into the phone.

"*Ahhhhhh!*" my mom shrieked back.

Both of us made weird squealing noises into the phone for several minutes, unable to contain the thrill of finally achieving a long-awaited win.

Eventually we regained our composure. "Go tell your father! I'll be home soon. I am so proud of you, Bruce!" The sounds of those words were so genuine that they seemed visible from my end of the phone line.

At an Olympic pace, I ran back the exact route I had just taken and busted through my dad's shop door to deliver the news. "*Dad, I got the role of Oliver!*" He was tied up in his work, literally, bundling rods with string, but he stopped what he was doing to give me a hug and reward me with a cup of hot cocoa. At home that night, his always delicious cooking seemed flavored with an extra dash of fatherly pride.

As I reflect on those months, I see that my life had become a never-ending cycle of school, drive, rehearsal, drive. I was getting home at 9, 10, or even 11 o'clock, then sleeping a few hours before getting up and repeating the same schedule the following day. I would scribble out my homework, wherever and whenever I could, usually on the drives to and from rehearsal. I was also taking band at school and was learning to play the clarinet in the only available practice space, my mom's car on the way to the theatre.

As the show date neared, the publicity increased. There were releases to the press, advertisements in newspapers, snippets of the show performed at area conferences, and of course appearances on local TV and radio. I was in the limelight, bathed in a sense of exhilaration, and a growing intimidation. Surreal moments punctuated otherwise mundane events, like grocery shopping at Walmart, where I was recognized by a stranger as the kid who was playing Oliver.

I relished my newfound fame. It all started to feel real. I could sense the pressure and expectations rising, but I still loved this new world.

The growing notoriety didn't completely absolve me of my previous challenges with bullies. One day in the school lunchroom, a very popular older boy named Trevor taunted me with cruel remarks from across the lunch tables. "He is so gay, the little theatre boy."

Then, out of nowhere, his social equal, a popular girl in school named Kathleen, stood up and snapped back, "Are you kidding me, Trevor!? Don't you know that Bruce is kind of famous in the theatre in Butte? Do you know how many girls are in theatre that swoon over the leading actor of a play? I bet you Bruce has more girls than you do!" she said calmly yet assertively. Kathleen was in her junior year and was genuinely liked by everyone. She stood her ground and faced him dead on, which caused him to clam up. He never said another word about me or to me from that point forward, at least not to my face.

Amidst the anticipation of opening weekend at the Mother Lode, moments of doubt and insecurity were creeping in. Following the final dress rehearsal, my mom and I got into the car to make our way back over the mountains that separated Butte from Twin Bridges. Tears streamed down my face. I was panicked. The fear of failure, the weight of expectation had supplanted my youthful enthusiasm.

"I can't do it. I can't do this," I began to explain to my mother, hoping my protest would allow me a means of escape.

"Well, it's a little late now for that now," she replied. "Just breathe. You are going to be okay, and you are going to be great. Just breathe." She was right. I just needed to breathe and do what I had been training for over the past few months. My confidence returned.

The audience was electric. I could feel the energy of the large and lively crowd. My cheeks were warmed in the spotlight. With each performance as the star of the show, my addiction to theatre grew. I loved every second.

The success of the show, and seeing me comfortable, free, and flourishing for the first time, encouraged my parents. When they heard that an audition for the national tour of *Oliver!* was being held in New York City, they knew we needed to seize the opportunity. Two months passed, then my dad and I packed and headed out. *This is my chance to go to the Big Apple!* I was six when I had received a postcard with a picture of New York from my birth mother. It had captured my imagination and sparked my dream to one day live in such an exciting place.

Now, stepping off the plane in Newark, New Jersey, was pure joy, like being deluged with a million winning lottery tickets. I thought my heart might explode. I already wanted more, more of the energy, more of the adventure, more of the unknown possibilities that lay just across the Hudson.

A family friend, Christiane, who lived in Twin Bridges, Montana, also lived part time in New Jersey. She was awaiting our arrival at the airport. We would be staying in her home, a stunning colonial mansion with an Escher painting's worth of stairs connecting its maze of rooms.

That night we ate dinner together as my obsession with anything New York related was building. I was captivated by their salt and pepper shakers, which were little replicas of the Chrysler Building and the Empire State Building. The excitement of the whole experience made me certain of one thing: someday I would live in that city of novelty and wonder.

After dinner, when the night started to wind down, my father moved me in the direction of bedtime. We had a very busy day ahead of us and I needed to be rested. I remember lying in bed staring out the window, just looking at the city lights. *I am here. I have made it.*

A very early knock on the door awakened me. "Time to go hit the big city!" my dad called. I shot out of bed, rocketing toward my awaiting adventure. "Today is the day!" I cried out with joy. I hastily pulled on my clothes before dashing down the stairs.

Excitement radiated from my body as we waited for the bus and rode into New York. We exited into the hustle of 42nd Street in front of the Port Authority Bus Terminal, just a few blocks from Times Square. I looked around, first at the towering buildings and then with determination into the eyes of my father. "I am going to live here," I proclaimed.

Our fun began with taking in the buzz and bustle of a brisk Midtown morning. We whirled through Times Square, took photos on the steps of Carnegie Hall, and even ate a hot dog from a street vendor as steam billowed from his cart. The city was an endless swirl of energy, where steam even rose out of vents in the busy streets and sidewalks.

Taxi here, taxi there, then an afternoon meandering the snow-covered trails in Central Park.

Montana's pristine drifts were pure white, but New York's millions of cars and people quickly turned it into slushy black muck. We ended our day by walking back through Times Square at night before heading to the Empire State Building for a sweeping aerial view of this vibrant city. From above the grit and grime and the clang and clamor of the streets below, I developed a silent sense of belonging. I felt safe and connected.

The next day was audition day and I was getting nervous. I was five foot one and they were only looking for boys under five feet, so I decided to slouch. The casting directors saw through my little plan, but when they saw that I had played the leading role previously, they let me audition.

The true performer in me kicked in. My nerves melted away and I turned on the charm. Despite dazzling them with my rendition of "Consider Yourself" and then nailing the choreography during the dance call, I was cut due to my height. However, I felt no sadness. In my mind, I had already won, simply being in New York City and having my first audition. My dream had already come true, and the future was mine, or so I thought.

After the fun-filled days in New York, I returned to school in Twin Bridges, a place I hated. The disdain I now felt was exaggerated by the passion I felt for New York. Part of the pace followed me as I performed in a series of shows at the community theatre in Butte over the next few years. Summers were alive with performances in the repertory theatre of the Virginia City Players. I was proud of the paychecks. *I was a professional actor.* But the time spent on the roads became a burden. With the relentless commuting back and forth for shows and rehearsals, my parents quickly tired of the chauffeuring to Butte.

They had also become fed up with the school system in Twin Bridges doing absolutely nothing about the ruthless bullying.

It was time to move again. My parents put our beautiful craftsman home on the market and began to look for houses in Butte. On the brink of this change, I was also experiencing some internal changes as well, but I was oblivious to their dangers. I was now 13 or 14 years old and very much in puberty. My developing mind and body were a-rage with testosterone.

A late-night habit had been formed. I would sneak out of my room and pass the darkest hours of the night ingesting internet porn on the family computer. This was the innocent start of my sex addiction. The more I watched, the more my compulsion progressed. I yearned for a male partner. I fantasized about the boys in my school and the boys at the theatre. They all claimed to be straight. *Or so they said*. It was driving me nuts. The frustration grew with each hormone-assaulted day. I needed an escape.

I had an example of one potential path of escape in my own family at the time. One of my sisters had attempted suicide and had been hospitalized and then sent to a group home to recover. The process took years. But I was looking for a different way out. I didn't want to die, but I needed to flee.

Twenty aspirin. That was my attempt. But the desperation of that moment quickly passed as I told my parents what I had just done. They immediately rushed me to the hospital in Sheridan, the closest one. Medical staff pumped my stomach and decided it was best that I get immediate professional help. Like my early therapy sessions, I was unable to communicate what was really going on. Instead, I lied and said that I wanted to kill myself. So I was sent to a children's hospital called Shodair in Helena, Montana. It was during my week-and-a-half stay in the acute unit, that I was first diagnosed with bipolar 1.

They then transferred me to Kids Behavioral Health (KBH) in Butte, where I stayed for another five months.

There in KBH I experienced my first *consenting* sexual activity with another boy. Not anything adult—rather, my first kiss and some innocent, passionate groping that never went further.

Upon my discharge from the center, my parents brought me to our new house, a very nice midcentury home tucked on the hillside known as Big Butte. Butte was a rough and rugged type of town, heavy with a population of Irish Catholics. In its prime, during the copper mining days of the mid- to late 1800s, Butte was teaming with a population of over 150,000 hearty people. When we moved there it had just 30,000, all living under the threat that the mile-deep mining pit at its center might burst and flood the lower portions of town with a stew of toxic runoff.

Time changes everything. I had gone from a town of 300 people to a junior high that had over 400. My new school was private and Catholic, but nobody cared that I was gay. My teachers and peers were accepting and welcoming. For the first time in my entire life, I wasn't bullied.

I continued performing with the local community theatres in and around Butte during the years that followed. In this safe haven, I would be introduced to a new home-away-from-home, called Same Difference Inclusive Theatre Company, created and run by an incredible woman named Mellie. Mellie would later become known as "my other mother" due to the incredible amount of time I spent with her and her children.

Same Difference was a theatre company that included anyone who had, or didn't have, any kind of physical or mental disability. Thanks to this unique company, I was getting more than just the chance to perform, or even a community of companions, I was receiving an education in acceptance. I learned more there about humankind and how to relate than I had in any other area of my life. I discovered the wisdom that lies in refraining from judgment based on appearances or limitations, and that encountering difference is a strength.

For instance, my fellow performers and I had all been bullied for different reasons, but in that difference was a commonality that allowed us to form pure, unconditional, honest friendships with one another. While some had physical disabilities, I had unseen cognitive learning disabilities brought on by fetal alcohol effects, but none of us were greater or weaker because of who we were, how we identified, nor whether we had a disability. What mattered was how we could love others and ourselves.

With the clarity I learned in Same Difference, I came to realize that my life was my own and need not be dictated by the whims of others. I was at the reins, with the ability to chart my own course. No matter what anyone had to say or think about us, we were all equally beautiful and the same in our unique ways. We would get to decide how we would navigate the waters of our own lives. It is truly all the same difference.

Breathe. I am capable of being myself and can step into my light, despite how difficult it may be. I am capable.

Breathe. With great success comes the temptation to ruin it, but I don't have to.

Breathe. We are all the same in many different ways. I am a part of the same difference.

Breathe. I can and will move forward.

---

6 | The Foot That Should Have Kicked Me

Breathe. When your trusted few provide a warning, listen. Be careful of ego. When you think you know it all, think again. Getting away with something in the moment doesn't mean you will escape the consequences later.

Breathe. When you start to gain speed, spinning faster and faster, slow down so you can see where you're headed.

Breathe. Remember that temptation isn't need.

Breathe. Keep moving forward.

What a relief to be in a new school where bullying was prohibited and consequences for violating the policy were enforced. Free from my old classmates' toxic behavior, I was flourishing. I soared through my classes, passing every course with excellent grades, surprising both myself and my parents. The possibilities for me had suddenly opened.

As a bonus, the dress code that other students bemoaned, I embraced. Our private school required blazers, which I picked out with glee every morning and paired with complementary shoes and trousers. I felt well dressed and well liked, making friends easily for the first time.

I was thriving in my new school. After years as an outcast, I enjoyed a bit of popularity among my peers. I studied the way I should have and achieved grades that matched my efforts. As my confidence increased, so did the amount I was able to accomplish. In a positive feedback loop, those accomplishments helped to bolster my wounded self-esteem. I exceeded the requirements, finishing out my first year there by writing and producing a play called "Light on the Street," in which my drama club peers served as actors. It told the story of a fictional family in Germany during World War II. After being killed in the war, the father returned to communicate to his children through a lamppost on the street where they lived. Nightly, the orphans would sneak out to receive the coded messages from their missing parent through the light. Not only did I love the play that I had created, but I also loved the fact that so many members of the city of Butte came to see it: peers, teachers, neighbors, strangers, and friends. The play, the actors, and my efforts received glowing reviews throughout the community. The positive response ended my school year with a bang.

In the summer, I worked with my mom in her best friend Judy's candy store. In previous summers, I had hung around as an unofficial volunteer, but that summer I was finally old enough to work alongside my mom as a real employee. I kneaded my way through the summer months, making hundreds of pounds of saltwater taffy to fill the wooden barrels that lined the shop's display. Virginia City, Montana, where the store was located, is nestled in the Greenhorn Mountains and looks like it has been preserved since the Gold Rush era.

The shop's antique decor was like something out of *Little House on the Prairie*, and its bins and barrels overflowed with every imaginable old-time treat.

Several of my close theatre friends from Butte also worked in the shop. Nicole was a few years older than me and quite the rebel. Jancee was striking, with an effervescent personality. Lovely Kathleen, who had stood up for me in the lunchroom, had warm, radiant eyes and a demeanor to match. She was the assistant manager and watched over my sister Megan and me, who were usually working together.

During breaks from our busy days at the shop, we would wander down to the Virginia City Players on one side of town and the Brewery Follies on the other. They first offered a rotating family-friendly presentation of "varied vigorous vagary of vivacious vaudeville variety acts," while the latter boasted a risqué banquet of adult cabaret. We couldn't get enough of either, and in the case of the Follies, we were the only kids allowed thanks to a scheme we repeated frequently: we stuffed our pockets with candy from the shop—our version of a golden ticket—and bartered for free entrance to the shows. While the shows rarely changed, we didn't care; they were the best entertainment our young eyes had ever seen. The casts, from all over the United States, were stars in our eyes. After the performances, we often headed to the Bale of Hay Saloon to hang out and gossip. Other nights we could be found down behind the opera house where the actors had their housing. There would always be a bonfire and we would sing and tell stories until late at night. It was absolutely the best time in my life, until one fateful day nearly closed the curtains.

Behind the candy shop was a tall iron ladder that squeezed through a very narrow, vertical access point to the top of the building. My friends and I had claimed the private rooftop as our own, and often gathered there on our lunchbreaks and after work. One bright morning we took in the clear view and filled the rooftop with our boisterous teenage laughter. Caught in the energy of the moment, I whirled like a dervish in a wild dance, like I had so many times before. It was a harmless, silly way to vent my high-wire energy. The roof was made of metal and punctuated by camouflaged vents. I danced high and low, spinning and turning, barely conscious of the dangers lurking underfoot. I joyously spun, quickly and forcefully throwing my leg outward in a wild move as I twisted around. *Thwack!* I dropped instantly. I had hit the top of my foot on a sharp edge of metal flashing. My entire body collapsed as I hugged my foot tightly.

The metal had sliced through the flesh far more deeply than I had expected. I rocked back and forth in excruciating pain with both my hands pressed firmly on the top of my foot. As I did, blood started to pulse out between my fingers in a sickening syncopation with the beat of my heart. The cut was so deep that my artery was split and four tendons were severed.

My sister Megan shouted for Jancee to get help and then shouted for me to look away. She ripped off her shirt and tightly wrapped my foot to slow the bleeding. I tried to stand for the short walk to the ladder but promptly fell back down. Trying to walk was useless without my tendons. Since I was in shock, I don't remember the pain nearly as much as feeling tingly and extremely faint, which is unsurprising given the amount of blood that was being pushed out of my body. Hands and knees were my only option, so I crawled toward the ladder. Peering to the ground two stories below, I sensed a certain tragedy just moments in the future, but had no option but to try. I placed one knee on the first rung and began the precarious descent.

Meanwhile, Jancee was panicking, trying to get my mom's attention, but my mom was unfazed, having dealt with more than one instance of children overreacting to scrapes and scratches. Unhurried, she patiently reminded Jancee of the odd jobs that needed attending to around the store, then she headed out back to deal with what she expected would be a minor injury.

Upon seeing my mangled foot, she immediately realized it was serious, but she managed to keep her cool. She grabbed her purse, keys, and a towel, and then helped me into the front seat of her car. "Don't bleed on the leather," she said half-joking, perhaps trying to calm me down, or perhaps to keep herself focused on what she needed to do.

The nearest medical facility was a small clinic 14 miles away over a mountain pass. The doctors there confirmed that I had cut an artery and needed to be taken to the big hospital in Butte for immediate surgery. They cauterized the artery to stop the gushing blood, then we got back in the car and rushed to Butte for a four-hour surgery.

Instead of continuing my fun, I was essentially bedridden for the rest of the summer. I started freshman year on crutches and in a medical boot. The barrage of inquiries about what had happened allowed for a little harmless lying, so I spun a tale of intrigue: "I was on a movie set as a stunt double and it went horribly wrong!"

"Wow, really? What movie?" they would probe, gathering closer, eager for all the gory details. Once I had their attention, I would confess and relate the true sequence of events, which proved even more horrifying.

As I made new friends, I also made new enemies among the big sharks at the top. On top of that, my wild hormones were not helping my social adjustment. I was fighting an incessant desire for the cute boys with perfect bodies that seemed to pass me at every corner of the hallways. Gym class was likely to make me faint faster than the loss of blood during my foot fiasco. Youthful desire and curiosity sparked in me in ways that I simply did not need at that moment.

I had no outlet to express my sexual desires. There was no way I was going to talk to my parents or my female therapist about it. At the very least, I wanted to talk it out with someone who was like me, who would fully understand. I also fantasized about having sex with a gay boy like me who would share my feelings. However, neither of these was an option, and I don't think that it would have helped me anyway, so I just stuck with what I knew best, sneaking out of my room to use the family computer to watch internet porn, which I did for the remainder of my freshman year. My exploits ruined four family computers, but did not extinguish my enflamed addiction.

In my sophomore year, I acquired a driver's license, but not common sense. I feared the humiliation of getting caught again, so I formulated an ill-conceived plan to put an end to my late-night secret: I would steal my parents' car after they had gone to bed! Then I could head downtown to Hastings, a cafe and general store that was open late. My goal: to shoplift their porn magazines. These I could keep in my room under my mattress so that I could stop using the family computer. If only the light bulb of insight that flashed briefly through my head one night had blown a fuse and short-circuited my plan. Instead, my attempt to avoid one transgression by engaging in another only compounded my mischief. After that first success stealing porn from Hastings, my cockiness grew. I continued to get away with it and before long, I was not only stealing internet time and magazines, but also the family car and money from my parents' wallets.

After the first theft of my parents' car, this spiraled into a regular pattern. When I wasn't procuring porn, I was joyriding around Butte at all hours of the night. Sometimes, when I wasn't stealing dirty magazines, I took a high school friend on my escapades, and other times she would pick me up for a late-night sojourn at Taco John's before they closed at 1 a.m. If not for the Grand Theft Auto element, it would have been innocent teenage fun. After binging on burritos, we would head to her house and chuckle our way into the wee hours laughing at *I Love Lucy* on VHS.

One night, in the midst of my ill-begotten but now familiar routine, I veered my mom's car off of one of the exits on the interstate that passed through our town. I slowed to a stop before a red light, being extra careful to obey all the traffic laws. It was about midnight when across the intersection, I glimpsed a familiar car. It was my dad. *Shit! I've been caught!* The light turned green, and I pressed on the gas so hard that the pedal hit the floor. My dad was right on my tail. I screeched through a hard left, ignoring the red light and hoping fate was on my side. I was flying, going nearly 60 miles per hour down a street with a speed limit of 25, desperate to get away from him, even though I would have to go home eventually and face the consequences. My escapades in search of porn had morphed into a high-speed chase. Fearlessly matching my speed, my dad floored it until he had pulled his car up alongside me. His steely eyes glared directly into my soul as he shouted, "Pull over!" and pointed to the side of the road.

My defeat was obvious. After several futile seconds of trying to think my way out of this self-made predicament, I slowed the car down and pulled over. There was no way out, and I knew it.

We left my mom's car by the side of the road and I got in his. Not one word was spoken the entire way, the silence filled only with the deafening beat of my heart. The silence continued until we reached home. When we got to the front stairs of the house, all he said was "Go to bed." Mom had probably been the one to send him to look for me. My parents delivered my punishment the next day: my driving privileges were gone, and I was grounded—a rare consequence in our house.

As the weeks passed, my desires and my yearning to find a male who was like me didn't dissipate; they increased. The more intense my preoccupations, the more frequent my escapades. I got really good at stealing adult magazines from stores. I also got really good at being sly and stealthy, using school computers for illicit purposes during the daytime, during school hours. Once, I even used the computers at Montana Tech's library to print adult images, running to the printer to retrieve the contraband and shove it in my backpack, leaving the librarians none the wiser.

Not all of my plans were covert. I once cheekily entered the local adult novelty store, where the woman behind the desk questioned my age but didn't care enough to kick me out. Given my baby face, I must have been convincing when I told her I was 18. She even sold me five DVDs. The imaginary wall of the films was broken when I started to call the sex hotlines advertised at the start of the videos. That was the tipping point for me. I made a barrage of connections with desperate men across the nation, which gave me the green light to plan my escape. I had entered the deep end. I loved the thrill of mischief and behaving as I pleased, consequences be damned.

As my sophomore school year came to a close, so did my stable mental health. I was running nowhere, very fast. The repercussions from the trauma of my early life were starting to creep into my confused adolescent brain, and they affected my thinking, encouraging me to act out. The welcome reprieve from those horrendous first years had been short-lived. Mom and Dad had shown us the world, given us love and support, and kept my sisters and me together, but they couldn't vanquish the monsters that had been hiding in my mind.

Breathe. I must be careful of ego. When I think I know it all, I need to think again. Getting away with something in the moment doesn't mean that I will escape the consequences later.

Breathe. When I start to gain speed, spinning faster and faster, I will slow down so I can see where I'm headed.

Breathe. I will remember that temptation isn't need.

Breathe. I can and will keep moving forward.

7

The Runaway

Breathe. If you latch onto anger, and stay content with that anger, you will remain angry. If you latch onto joy, and stay content with that joy, you will remain joyous.

Breathe. What doesn't belong to you, doesn't belong to you.

Breathe. It is better to jump into a world you are vaguely familiar with than one you know nothing about.

Breathe. Keep moving forward.

Montana summers can get hot, and it was one of those days in Virginia City. Hundreds of tourists walked the refurbished boardwalks of the ancient mining town, and it seemed like every single one of them had decided to come into our candy shop for the frigid air conditioning and free samples of our famous saltwater taffy. The taffy puller was strategically placed in the center of the large picture window at the front of the store. There was no escaping the beckoning of a little sweet indulgence. So they came. And on this day, in my usual position manning the taffy puller, I had reached my capacity.

The parade of cute faces squashed against the glass, peering in with mouths agape and hypnotized lollipop eyes made me squeamish. The sweet smell of the fudge was sickening and heightened by my simmering agitation. Even the tourists' foreign languages, which I normally found fascinating, annoyed me as the cryptic words battered my ears.

My mood had been off the previous few weeks. It was the summer following my sophomore year, and I had latched onto feelings of anger and resentment. I had withdrawn from my friends and family due to my mental health, all the while becoming more comfortable in self-isolation. The times that I did feel happiness—or what I labeled as happiness—was when I was away from them. When they were around, I felt judged and unworthy. I imagined that, in their estimation, I was fucking up in every regard. In secrecy, I was continuing inappropriate fantasy relationships I had formed with much older men online, and my old life was slipping away. I wasn't cast in that summer's season of shows because I had called out frequently so that I could go to the library to watch porn instead of showing up for my scheduled performances.

I was lying and stealing candy, which seems fairly innocent compared with other things I was up to. And that particular transgression was nothing new. When I was seven or eight, I had snuck out of my room to forage for my mom's secret candies, which she stashed high in the cupboard of the laundry room. I shut the door behind me as I entered, trying to keep quiet so no one would hear, but I inadvertently locked myself in. I banged and banged, but no one came to my rescue. It wasn't until my prepubescent high-C shriek pierced through the house that my parents finally found me and opened the door.

Then, buck naked, I flew past and ran straight back to my room. When they came in and asked if I had stolen candy, I lied through my chocolate-covered teeth. With my cheeks stuffed with Reese's, I denied everything. Episodes like this got me labeled an incurable liar.

My parents may have been trying to help me become a better person. They were fully aware of my continual lying and stealing, and tried to correct my shortcomings by constantly pointing them out. Perhaps they hoped I would be ashamed of my behavior and that would prompt a positive change. But I was not ashamed, and the endless tough love was not working. Instead, I was actively fantasizing about taking on the persona of a bad boy. The normally playful, boisterous Bruce had become very cold and distant. I didn't even recognize myself. My moods were erratic, swinging from manic extremes to vacant, emotionless numbness. I felt as if I was on the verge of crying but never could produce any tears. The last time I had cried was when my oldest sisters had been sent away as teenagers after my parents struggled to help them cope with serious mental and physical difficulties. It was all my parents knew to do, and the therapists agreed that it would be best to send them away for more intense care. What it said to me was that we were easily discarded, that we had never really been wanted. That we really had no permanent, safe space. They didn't love us and they wouldn't keep us. Even though I didn't fully believe this, it stoked my abandonment issues, and in some regard it gave me an excuse to latch onto anger, whether or not it was justified.

But before all this anger, before this madness of emotions that I couldn't label and didn't understand, I had cried for my sisters. Filled with genuine empathy, I had cried out of fear that they would never find genuine love, for themselves or for others. I had worried that they would repeat Berna's piteous choices, or die far too young. But I hadn't cried for myself, and I didn't that blazing summer, no matter how much I may have needed catharsis. Instead, I had this, whatever *this* was.

To complicate my chaotic pattern of intense and absent emotions, I felt incredible frustration from my own lack of emotional control and predictability. Little things, like carelessly dropping a piece of merchandise or my mother asking me to help with a chore, resulted in big outbursts. Every time, my anger would spike cosmically out of scale. Other times I would look in the mirror through vacant eyes and see nothing staring back at me. I felt hollow, disconnected from reality, and from authentically feeling my emotions. I could also make others who were looking at me think that nothing was wrong. My acting chops had been honed, and now I could fake it with the best of 'em. In my delusion I thought that precious few knew what a mess I was on the inside. It was obvious to everyone, but I thought that barely anyone knew that I was slowly losing my mind, becoming hateful, and running headlong toward the path of self-destruction.

It was halfway through my shift when my mother approached me with a list of things that needed to be done before we closed shop for the day. Countless candies needed to be carried upstairs, unboxed, sorted, inventoried, and then put on the shelves and into the display cases. The chocolates needed to be weighed, bagged, and labeled. The whole shop needed to be dusted, swept, and mopped. And then, inevitably, it would all need to be done again because, as always, a new gaggle of tourists would waddle through, trudging dirt into the store and discarding sample wrappers everywhere.

As the mundane list of chores rolled off my mother's lips, my own lips took up a different activity. I softly started singing to myself, tuning her out! This was a mistake.

Furious, she stomped over and started to spray me with a bottle of Windex. She held her composure fairly well given the powder keg of stress she was under. "*Shhh!* Stop it! Stop it! Stop it, Bruce! What has gotten into you? *Listen to me!*" she demanded, enraged by my rudeness.

That was it. Our insignificant little altercation was the last rational moment I remember before completely shutting off mentally. I was no longer in control of my impulses. I threw the mop on the floor.

"Well, good luck finding someone to finish your little list. I quit!" I replied with a bitter bark. I barged down the stairs to the employee bedroom, a space shared by three to six of the shop's teenage workers who drove in from hours away and worked long shifts. I had been staying there too, that summer. In happier moments, the area was like a joyous camp, but now it was just another dark, cold, damp basement. I flailed about, wildly packing all my belongings.

"Fuck her . . . fuck this . . ." I kept saying as I threw my things into a large suitcase.

Soon after, sure enough, my mother came downstairs. "Get your things. Get in the car. I am driving you home," she swiftly stated, pointing at me intently.

We sat in screaming silence until the car had reached the end of town. Her tactic changed. She tried to break the awkwardness. "Please don't do this. Stay just a few more weeks. The season is almost over!"

"No," I mumbled.

She stopped the car. "My mother is in hospice, Bruce. I need to be able to fly away at any moment to see her before she dies, and I won't be able to do that if you aren't working." Her tone was rational and calm, but sharp.

I slowly turned toward her, my voice becoming firmer and more pointed. "No. Now, are you going to drive or am I?" I said with the hint of a dirty smirk on my face.

The rest of the drive was an hour and a half of unsettling quiet, with my mother steaming silently beside me.

Out my window, the gorgeous green of the valleys and the dark blue of the mountains gave off a sense of calm. It reflected what someone might have seen peering in through the car window at our motionless forms. But despite my stillness, chaos raged in my mind and chest.

My father was waiting on the doorstep with a concerned look in his eyes, his arms crossed over his stomach. The tension between my mother and me quickly enveloped him. "Go inside and leave your bags at the top of the stairs," my mother commanded.

I rolled my eyes, and continued walking past my father without even acknowledging he was there. I felt his eyes on me the whole time, riddled with confusion and anger. This wasn't just about my outburst at the candy shop. There was more. He knew. They knew. I had stolen money from the store's register earlier that day and I was certain they had caught on. I remember thinking to myself, "They're no dummies, dammit!" My ruse had been going on for nearly a week. I was never supposed to handle the money, but when others were preoccupied or no one was around, I would swipe cash from the register.

In this instance, I did as I was told and marched to the top of the stairs, where I dropped my bags. I snuck a quick look over my shoulder to ensure they were not watching. They were engrossed in intense whispering back and forth on the porch, most likely developing a plan to discipline me.

I saw my chance and reached into my bag to the envelope containing several hundred dollars of stolen money. This was my ticket to the world of freedom I had been craving for months.

I slipped the stash into my underwear, well aware they would rummage through my bags, but assuming they wouldn't strip search me. I had only just pulled down my shirt to further conceal the envelope when my parents burst in. My mother dived into my bags. She was visibly upset but maintained her cool as she navigated the crevasses of my bag in hopes of finding the stolen cash. Her excavation turned up nothing!

My father turned to the suitcase. Inside, he found and confiscated my paycheck for $400, giving it to my mother, who immediately took it to their bedroom at the top of the stairs. No matter. I would still have enough in stolen cash to get to another city and have money for food when I got there—wherever *there* was.

Moments later she returned empty-handed but with a new, earnest intent. "Bruce!" she said to me. "We know that you have more, and if you don't hand it over right now, we will be pressing charges for theft." To emphasize the seriousness, she lowered her chin. This allowed her to pierce her glare directly into my eyes with the sharp edge of her square-rimmed glasses acting as a barbed-wire fence between us. "We can get the police involved now and have them search everything if you prefer that." Sarcasm tinged her tone, with a bit of a shake working its way into her body language as well.

I did not want the police involved. If they came and searched, they would find a small bag of weed that some friends had given me. Ironically, at that point, I didn't even like drugs or alcohol. In a twisted way, being around it made me feel bad. I thought that drugs were bad and alcohol was stupid. It reminded me of Berna, someone I wanted to be nothing like. The couple of times I had tried weed were simply misguided attempts at rebellion, small ways to fit in. I hated it, and I hated smoking. On those few occasions when I had lit a cigarette, I took a little smoke in my mouth, but didn't inhale, so my friends wouldn't catch on. Now here I was, with a bit of unwanted contraband that had been sitting around for months, unsmoked, in place to foil my escape.

To avoid catastrophe with the police, I whipped the envelope of stolen cash out of my pants and hurled it at my parents.

"Happy?" I blurted in the rudest tone I could conjure, one worthy of an early '90s PSA. I slid my way past them and stormed downstairs in a rage. Fueled with adrenaline, I slammed the door to my room, feeling pressure build inside me. Blood pounded through my veins. How the fuck am I going to get that money back? My silent internal screams were building into a volatile hysteria. The explosion was imminent.

Then I heard the front screen door slam shut. Had my parents gone back outside? They had. It wasn't too late. I could get the money back and escape.

As the clock ticked, I hatched a hasty plan. I grabbed my shoulder bag and threw in some clothing, music, the bag of weed, some leftover makeup that I had from my numerous plays, and a journal—an unlikely item since I hated to write. But for some reason I felt compelled now. On a piece of paper I scrawled, in all capital letters:

YOU WILL NEVER UNDERSTAND ME! YOU WILL NEVER LOVE ME AND I DON'T WANT YOUR LOVE! I WOULD RATHER BE DEAD THAN KNOW YOU BOTH! DON'T TRY FINDING ME! I AM LEAVING AND I AM NEVER COMING BACK! YOU WILL NEVER FIND ME!

The chaos of emotions and biology was a multilayered screen in my mind. Leaving the note on my bed, I frantically tried to think of the next step. I stealthily opened my door and made my way to the upstairs landing, where I passed my parents on the front porch. Their hushed tones couldn't cover their intense distress. They were perplexed and searching, feeling powerless to advance a plan that was both urgent and long out of reach.

"He is mentally ill!" "He is delusional!"

I ignored their comments and realized that I could slip past them. I tiptoed into my parents' bedroom. *How stupid!* I thought. There on the bed, in plain sight, was the envelope of stolen money. My desperate, thieving hands grabbed the stash. I dashed back to my bedroom and locked the door behind me.

I remember the pounding of my heart and the screaming of my mind. Thoughts, thousands of fragmented thoughts. A marathon of misperception. A muddle of nonsense. A babble devoid of reason, mixed with a touch of thrill. The surge and the rush of living on the dangerous side. It felt intoxicating. Darkness beckoned with a wrecking excitement.

They won't catch me! They are not going to get me! Not this time! I jumped out of the window, bag slung over my shoulder, and disappeared into the night.

Like many children, I had made several "cute" runaway attempts before. As a boy of five, for reasons I don't remember but suspect involved being denied ice cream, I had packed up my cartoon backpack with candies for food and headed out. The "faraway" place my child mind had chosen was Sheridan, the last place we had lived with Berna. Perhaps that was a subconscious cry to go back to the time before everything changed, but that is simply speculation. This first attempt at leaving involved a walk along the road out of town in the direction of my first home. I stopped at the local gas station to deposit five cents in the gumball machine to get extra "food" for the journey. Not long after that, Kathleen's mother saw me by the side of the road. After I refused her ride home, she immediately drove the short distance to get my father to come pick me up.

■ ■ ■

I made my way down the hill, across our neighbor's driveway, and into the cloak of night. All I knew was that I could not return home. I was done. I would keep moving forward and follow my impulse.

My friend Brooke lived only six blocks away. Each step in the direction of her house felt like a mini success. I walked up to the gate as her black lab barked wildly. My knocks on the door were met by her sister opening it with a surprised look. Nighttime visits were not the norm.

It didn't take much convincing for Brooke to give me a ride to the bus station.

The drive was short, and my confession likewise. "I'm running away," I calmly announced. "I'm actually going to do it!"

"Bruce! What? *No!*" Brooke insisted. "Will we hear from you again?" she asked innocently.

"*Ha!* Probably not!" I replied honestly.

Brooke had little more to say. After my second quiet and uncomfortable car ride of the day, we arrived at the Greyhound station.

I turned and faced my choice. *This is it, do or die time!* I looked at the doors to the station and walked inside. There was no one in sight except for a heavyset man in his mid-20s seated behind the bus station desk. He looked up, nonplussed.

"Can I help you?"

"Sure!" I replied. "I need a one-way ticket to . . ." I paused midsentence. *To where? Where the hell am I going to go? I am only 16 years old, for God's sake!* Then, for reasons unknown even to me, I blurted out, "Denver!" He raised one eyebrow. The Butte mentality was to ask no questions and give no fucks. It was a rough town. His blasé response was probably no more than a temporary bit of curiosity to ease his boredom. "Denver?" He mocked me, with doubt smearing his otherwise expressionless face. "Why does a boy like you want to be going to Denver, Colorado, at 12:30 a.m.?" he chuckled.

My impromptu explanation was the first in what would become an endless tumble of lies. "I was on vacation seeing family and vacation time is over. I'm going home!" I attempted an "attitude" to encourage believability. He shrugged his shoulders and started typing up my ticket. True to town, no fucks given.

What was in Denver? I had no clue! It was just the first big city to pop into my mind.

"Alright kid, what's your name?" The questions were basic, the lies were evolving.

"I'm sorry?" I asked, making it seem as if I had not heard him. I bought a moment to conjure a good alias.

"I said, what is your name, kid?" Disinterest morphed into irritability.

Again, I went with my first impulse and a name spun out of my mouth. "Todd Klein," I stated as I handed him the cash. He typed my new name into the computer and seconds later my ticket was printing. He handed it to me.

"Next bus is at 1:40 a.m.," he mumbled. I thanked him and walked back outside of the empty station.

I put my back against the wall and slid down until I was seated on the ground with my arms resting on my knees. There I waited for the bus to come to take me into a world I knew nothing about. I was giving up everything! Wherever my talents might have led, I was just throwing them away! The security of home, the stability of loved ones. "Fuck them!" I said out loud. I was literally insane in that moment.

My thinking was convoluted and wild. I was disassociated and acting out in ever more disturbing ways. The complexities of puberty and teenage socialization were amplified and out of control. I had previously outed my plan to run away to my parents multiple times in fanciful threats. I had told them that it would be better to sell myself as a sex slave and live with a stranger than to live with them. When they questioned how I would make money if I dropped out of school, I insisted I would find a millionaire. I was so delusional that I told them that I would have him pay for plastic surgery to change my face so they would never find me. Even this was tame compared to the episode when I wrote a death threat and placed it on the refrigerator for my mother to find. I needed help. I needed medication. But I wasn't prepared to listen. I wanted to find a solution to my pain on my own.

So here I was, slumped in the dirt, awaiting a bus. This time was for me. I kept reminding myself that I was my own and nobody else's. It was true, but in that context I was lost in out-of-tune static.

I latched onto the belief that *no one* would find me, and somehow this would be better. I would spread my wings, but where would I fly? I was jumping, expecting to soar, unaware that my wings were not yet developed and that an abyss existed just below the illusionary clouds. But, as they say, it's not the falling that kills you.

The nighttime quiet was broken by the sound of bus wheels heavy on the dirt and brakes squeaking as they slowed.

I was taking a big chance and I jumped into a world I did not know.

Breathe. If I latch onto anger, and stay content with that anger, I will remain angry. If I latch onto joy, and stay content with that joy, I will remain joyous.

Breathe. What doesn't belong to me doesn't belong to me.

Breathe. It's better to jump into a world I am vaguely familiar with than one I know nothing about.

Breathe. I can and will move forward.

8 | Journey to the Dream

Breathe. You can find comfort, even from a stranger.

Breathe. Obsessing over what you look like does not truly reflect what you are inside.

Breathe. Beware of thinking you are free rather than knowing you are free.

Breathe. Keep moving forward.

The bus was cold. The air conditioning was on too high. I had no warm clothes since it was the middle of summer.

As the bus drove toward I-90 East I pulled out the journal that I had taken from my room. I opened it and stared. The blank page invited me. Trying to find a way to start things off, I grasped my pen. I put its tip on the paper and I started to write.

I've done it. I am free. Watch me live. No one will anymore tell me how I am to live! I am my own!

I was overwhelmed with the feeling of power. It was a feeling I recognized only from success on stage and in art. My staccato heartbeat had calmed to its familiar resting rhythm. The night seemed endless as the tires of the bus rolled along the interstate pavement.

On my way, I wrote.

The sun announced the coming daytime by peeking over the mountains. My long, emotional night caught up with me, begging my heavy eyelids to close. Since I was the only one in my row, I lay down across both seats and curled into a ball. Without warning, I started to cry. I felt alone, scared, hopeless, and regretful. It was a brief moment of sanity that lasted long enough for me to wonder, *What had I gotten myself into?*

After what seemed to be hours, I fell asleep.

I woke up to the bus's breaks squealing. My body jolted up and my eyes instantly stretched open wide. I spun my head toward the front of the bus, clueless as to how long I had been asleep and where I even was! *What if I had missed my stop?!* The sun was towering above the mountains by this point. I looked out the window, hoping for a sign. And there it was: *Welcome to Billings*. Best I could tell, we had been driving for roughly six hours, making it sometime in the early morning.

Memories of the night before rushed over me like a torrent over a broken dam. I began to panic. *What did I do? What have I done?* I was lost and very confused, my mind tumbling over hundreds of thoughts piling up like a train derailing. *Where am I going? Where am I running too? Why am I running? How will I survive?*

And then, anger. Anger at everything—myself, my situation, my choices, my family—anger at the sun for coming up. My anger crystallized and a voice in my head told me that I would never be found. I had broken the law, not just by running away but also by stealing money from the candy store. I was a criminal now, but I was never going back.

"Shit, shit, shit!" I remember mumbling those words a lot. "Why do I always take the easy way out? It always turns out to be harder!" I whined to myself. Another moment of clarity.

My thoughts raced on as the bus came to a stop at the Greyhound station in downtown Billings. I had several hours before I would catch another bus to Denver. *Well, I've come this far, so I might as well keep going,* I told myself.

In my head, I doubted that my parents were even looking for me; I had pretended to run away so many times before. Part of me thought they would assume this was like the other times, and that I would return when I was hungry. But a small part of me worried that the police were already after me. This was the twinge of paranoia that would soon become a constant in my life.

This bus station resembled the Port Authority Bus Terminal in New York, but on a smaller scale. I walked out the main doors and turned left, where I found myself on the corner. A Denny's was just a few blocks farther. At diners, you don't pay until *after* you eat, so I could dine and ditch!

I crossed the street and headed toward the familiar red and yellow sign ahead. Consumed by thoughts of food, I did not notice the red Jeep Wrangler that had pulled up alongside of me. The driver, a middle-aged man with salt-and-pepper hair, leaned over and shouted at me through the passenger window, "You need a ride, cutie?"

The first thing to enter my mind were horror stories of girls and boys getting kidnapped, raped, and murdered. But my mind wasn't healthy, so the thought did not even faze me. I was becoming an adrenaline junky, and my head was crammed with porn fantasies. Instead, the thought of possible violence excited me in the way that people are drawn to explicit movies without considering what they mean in reality.

My hunger saved me from what could have been a disaster. I was lucky to have the bottomless appetite of a teenage boy. "No thanks!" I replied, "I'm just going to Denny's up the street."

As he drove off, my criminal mind scolded me for a missed opportunity. "Damn it! He could have paid me!" I mumbled to myself as I walked up to Denny's front door.

After dining and ditching, I caught my next bus. Several minutes after I boarded, I began to get exceedingly emotional. My moods dived and swung rapidly. At this point I was so distant from reality that I also believed I was invincible. I thought no one would hurt me like they had in the past, if I just moved forward. I had completely transformed from the loving and caring Bruce everyone was used to into a lonely and dissociated teenage runaway.

I did not care about anything. I was a creature who would fight for survival, and win, because I had no other option. It was as if I were an animal being sent back into the wild. Little did I know how wild things would get. My thoughts and emotions formed a tornado, and the pressures and desires that had caused my snap from reality spun slowly at the center. My decision to leave made me feel unbelievably powerful. Learning that I was sexually desirable to older men, as odious as it was, made me feel more beautiful than ever. I loved feeling this way. For once I was the person in control of my circumstances. If this was the only way to have it, I would have it. My future of addiction revealed itself, sinking its talons into this moment. I was addicted to this new and potent feeling. I would have killed for it.

An ever-changing landscape slid past the window during my day-long ride to Denver. My thoughts changed erratically, contradictory ideas that vacillated between being grounded and hyperbolically fatalistic. I was just as often pissed off, thinking about how bad a person I had become, unsure of running away despite what I told myself, but convinced I would never be loved again—not by my parents, not by my mentors, not by my friends or my community. On some level, I may have known that my parents loved me, but that thought couldn't surface in that moment. Some of my thoughts may even have been for their own dramatic sake. I couldn't be sure if I was lying to myself about what I believed and what I felt.

Inevitably, the muddled emotions would spiral downward, ending in fear. I feared that I would become lost in this world. I feared I would become a no-man, scum of the earth. *I would be better off dead.* The thought was a far cry from the invincibility I had felt just hours earlier. But if I was dead, I wouldn't have to deal with feeling the pain. I wouldn't have to feel like a crap kid.

The hours on the bus seemed endless. For a while, I sat next to an older gentleman whose head was crowned with tufts of silver hair. For three hours, he told me about how he had lost everything in his life: his family, his home, his job, and even his respect for himself. He had gone to prison for robbery, but I can't remember what he stole or why. I do remember that he had a Bible on his lap. When I look back, I realize that maybe he was trying to convey a message to spare me his own regrets. Maybe he was trying to tell me not to take anything for granted. Use what little you have and "make it huge" were his actual words. But it was not the right time for me to get help, nor did I want it.

The man got off the bus soon after we crossed the Colorado state line, but my destination was still hours away.

After several long hours of restless sleep and daydreaming, the skyline of Denver emerged from the horizon. "Now what?" I thought to myself.

I got up and walked to the bathroom in the back of the bus, closed the door behind me, and took out my makeup. I patiently applied black eyeliner, taking my time. Perhaps, subconsciously, I was just trying to mask my mess. But if I was going to feel beautiful, I needed to look beautiful. After I had drawn out the eyeliner into a smoky black effect around my upper eyelid, I applied mascara. I thought I looked stunning. In reality, I looked like a 16-year-old boy, with smeared makeup around his eyes, which were puffy from hours of crying. I was a wreck, I am sure, but I would never admit it at the time.

The bus pulled up to the station in downtown Denver and delivered me to yet another smelly, crowded bus station. Among the stream of people, I made eye contact with a boy with hair dyed platinum blond. His baby-blue V-neck T-shirt was nearly as tight as his dark-blue skinny jeans. Rainbow-colored bracelets lined his arms, so I assumed he too was gay. Seeing someone like me made me happy. I felt a flash of attraction, but when he smiled back, I could see that his teeth were black and many were missing. *He is so young! How did he do that to himself? Drugs?*

I was headed into the bathroom when paranoia hit. Two police officers were walking in my direction. I did not know whether they were after me, but there was no way I would be taking any chances. *I am never going home!* I froze, terrified and unsure what to do.

"*Shiiiiiiit!*" I screamed to myself. In a scene worthy of Laurel and Hardy, I slid frantically behind a man moving a cart of luggage and I followed, somewhat slouched alongside him to the front entrance to the station. My mind was working, but I was emotionally numb. I felt like I was working with four different brains, my personality flipping rapidly. I walked quickly to the corner, spooked by the near miss with the police. I approached a large man who was ambling about, and asked him where a kid like me would go to find some nightlife. He pointed me in the direction of a club that was close by. Without paying attention to where I was going, I thanked him and turned around briskly, swinging my duffel bag and bounding into the path of a girl, knocking her off balance and sending her and her luggage flying to the ground.

"Oh, my god! I am so sorry!" I apologized directly.

"No, it's alright. I wasn't paying attention either! I'm Tammy."

"I'm Todd."

She was on the shorter side, heavier set, originally from India and about 17. Her hair was out-of-control ratty, but her eyes were a rich brown and wide enough to cause envy in a Disney princess. I immediately found her fascinating.

I helped her pick herself up and gather her belongings. We walked together for a minute in the direction of the station. I had already completely forgotten about the police, enthralled with my new acquaintance. Our personalities were so alike. The once bubbly Bruce reappeared. Our connection was instant and we talked for the next hour in the waiting area, with barely a moment to breathe. She had been living in Denver for the last 18 months and was going back home to Tulsa.

This sparked another idea. Instead of Denver, I could go to Oklahoma City. Thoughts rushed through my head. I had been chatting online with a boy from Oklahoma City just a few weeks before running away. I would go and stay with him. Genius!

Lacking any other plan, a wave of excitement at this seemingly fortuitous encounter crashed over me. I excused myself and went up to the ticket counter. It cost $125 to get to Oklahoma City. My purchase put a major dent in the few hundred I had started with and I found myself in line yet again, preparing to board another aging, stinky, overcrowded bus. However, this time I had a traveling partner, Tammy, and a destination that had some sort of connection, however tenuous.

We found the last two adjoining seats, toward the back and on the left. It would be our oasis in a sea of crabby travelers. We settled in and descended into conversation while the bus sat at the gate. I peered outside to see if I could figure out the reason for our delay. Across the pavement, a group of policemen were moving in the direction of the bus. Immediately my blood began to boil. The hair on my neck prickled upward in instantaneous anxiety. I began to fidget as panic swept across me in a wave. I desperately tried to guess their intentions. *What should I do? Dash out the emergency exit? No, walk to the bathroom. Now.*

Futilely trying to appear calm, I crossed the aisle and slid into the bus bathroom. My gaze locked on my own eyes in the battered industrial mirror. *Wait. Don't breathe. Be silent.* I pleaded into the stagnant air for disappearance, either theirs or mine.

Unable to endure the intensity of the passing moments, nor to outwait my desperate curiosity, I fell into my own terror and opened the bathroom door to peek out. The officers were hovering in the aisle a few rows in front of where I had been sitting. My heart jumped into my throat. *No. How could this happen?* My mind ricocheted with fragments of thoughts and indecipherable emotions. *I am finished for sure!* Just as I was preparing to accept my capture, I heard deliberate steps moving to the front of the bus. Though muffled, the words were decipherable as the officer thanked the driver and exited. I couldn't believe it. I allowed another moment to pass then slipped out and hustled back to my seat.

Feigning ignorance, I asked Tammy, "Why was there a cop on the bus?"

"I wasn't really paying attention. I was listening to music. Why?" she replied, clueless to my information-gathering agenda.

"Just wondering," I said, quickly changing the topic. I had no plans to disclose my status as a runaway. Chameleon that I was becoming, I reentered our conversation where we had left off, willfully ignoring the sweat on my skin.

Several hours later, Tammy was asleep and so was everyone else, and I got an idea. Perhaps it was just to quell my boredom, or perhaps it was a way to purge the vortex of thoughts from my awareness. Perhaps it was a last physical connection to something tangible from home, or perhaps it was for no reason at all. I reached for the small bit of weed I had stashed in my bag. In the bathroom, I cracked the window and unceremoniously lit the small pipe. The victory of evil can enter even in a quiet moment. I inhaled. A journey of a thousand steps may begin with only one, but the direction matters.

The effect was felt, causing my gnawing hunger to intensify. Food was the only thing on my mind, other than sex, in just about any moment when my emotions weren't overwhelming me. Though still a virgin, I found that the compulsive desire for sex had become a massive problem. Lust was my higher power. Carnal fantasy was as omnipresent as breathing. Many teenagers who have entered the surge of puberty undergo some level of this, but my experience was something more insidious. It was like thinking, or dreaming, or having a heartbeat, I had no control over it. Rather, these unhealthy longings controlled me. I had no gay peers in Butte, and knowing my fantasies were impossible intensified them. I was hopelessly addicted and sickeningly in love with an illusion that I thought could only come true if I escaped. The worst part was that it had changed my natural way of thinking. I could not see the desperate situations I was creating and the destructive choices I was making.

And yet it was an unbelievable force of energy! At this point, two and two were not connecting. I loved it. I completely gave myself over to my addiction to sex and my naïve attempt to realize my sexual fantasies. What I couldn't see was that I had tricked myself into giving up a life that mattered. By running away, I had found a false sense of control.

I took another hit and had an inebriated epiphany while staring at myself in the bathroom mirror, my Narcissus pool. I remember thinking, *You're an attractive young boy. There are plenty of men who would love to have you and pay for it as well.* From that moment, I knew how I would make it on my own. I would sell my body for money. I would become a creature of the night, like the characters I idolized from movies and television.

Now that I felt like I was on a whole new mission, I started to obsess about my physical appearance. I had to be physically perfect. I could have no fat on my body. My incessant thoughts of food morphed as I turned to the toilet. I lifted the lid, sat on the floor, unconcerned with the grime, and without hesitation, I shoved my middle finger down my throat. I waited. Nothing. I did it again. Still nothing.

I looked around me and saw a pen that was on the sink counter. I grabbed it and jammed it down with force and determination. No delay—I threw up.

I have to stay perfect so men will want me. I am cute, I am willing, and I am ready. I am a gold mine. I thought to myself. I repeated the drastic ritual several more times until I thought I had thrown up enough. I stood and revisited my reflection. This time Narcissus's pool revealed a stream of tears. My makeup had smeared. *Good boy.* I told myself. *Good boy.*

I fixed my makeup and silently ambled back to my seat. The next lumbering hours on the bus revolved in a vain attempt to find sleep. Finally, I did, but the dark sleep that arrived was not rest. Before I ran away, my dreams had been a reliable route of escape, but this dream was a trap from which I couldn't wake up.

I found myself facing a door at the end of a suffocating, airless corridor. Escape would not be found by staying where I was. I moved forward, my trembling hand agonizing to find the handle. My fingers clasped around the knob. As I turned, its clicking sound echoed the dread resonating in my chest and off the walls of the desolate passage.

Rather than yielding slowly, the door swung open, releasing a chilling gust. Quivering, I ventured into a circular chamber that was immense in a way that defied physics. Its sinister grandeur was composed of ceilings soaring more than 40 feet and walls baring a soul-confining pattern of two-foot-wide stripes alternating between raven black and neon green, extending from floor to ceiling and evoking cage bars. The sole illumination for this unnatural chasm was the phosphorescent glow of the neon. Its dim, green pallor revealed a solitary chair at the center of the room. I was drawn inexplicably toward its presence and sat on its cold metal surface.

Suddenly, my peripheral vision caught the flicker of movement. A black object darted behind one of the neon stripes. My head whipped forcefully in that direction but there was nothing but a vacant void. I waited, my heart pounding. A clicking invaded my ear. Spooked and startled, I leapt to my feet, twirling around. Again, there was nothing.

Then, to my horror, a gaunt, towering silhouette of a man traversed from one neon green stripe to the next. It was as if the wall were a veil that the otherworldly figure existed behind. His form was traced in an unhallowed glow. He moved like fluid with an ethereal grace, as if in a trance or a dance. Then he started to change.

The man disappeared behind a black stripe, only to reappear as a tall, emaciated woman. She then continued to the next stripe, where her shape again morphed into male. With each passage across the stripe, the macabre form shifted between genders and emerged in a persistent and unsettling spectacle. After many repetitions, the silhouette fractured into twin apparitions and began running in opposing directions. The diabolical duo accelerated their pace from stripe to stripe, alternating in a nauseating succession.

Without warning, one of the silhouettes launched itself straight out of the wall and materialized, landing no more than an arm's length from my quivering frame. It was crouched in a feline manner, its sinewy limbs crawling slowly toward me. Its gait was unhurried, predatory. When it got close enough, it rose with deliberation. My eyes traveled up its elongating form with morbid fascination as it grew to a horrifying height of 13 feet. The mere 20-inch girth of its waist was a testament to an eternal hunger. Its meager 130 pounds glided in spite of its skeletal frame.

Its left arm jetted out to the side, revealing an ominous syringe with a long, thin needle at the tip, glinting menacingly. Suddenly, a blunt object knocked my body back into the chair. My limbs and torso were immediately ensnared by restraints that cut into my flesh, searing my nerves as I writhed. A scream tore from my throat, only to be sucked out and extinguished. My vocal chords were useless. My voice had been robbed.

The black stripes morphed into mirrors, in which I could see my own chilling reflection. I was in danger, teetering on the precipice of unspeakable peril.

The floor to my left began to shake, releasing a trap door and disgorging a cart. On it were three labeled boxes. "Brain" the first heralded. "Heart" the second taunted. "Voice Box" the third threatened. The damning truth clutched my soul. I did not want to admit it, but the reality was bare. My brain, heart, and voice box had been stolen and were now confined in these wretched vessels. I had become naught but a manipulated toy for a sadistic puppeteer.

The silhouette slithered close, assaulting me with the smell of decay as it bellowed at me.

"Do you know who I am?" my tormentor asked in a gravelly voice.

I frantically shook my head no, tears streaming down my face.

"I am your answers, your hopes, your dreams," it announced. "Do you know what is in this syringe?" Uninterested in concealing the smirk creeping across its face, it dared me to surrender to the fear engulfing my soul.

Again, I shook my head no.

Its laugh was maniacal. Its deranged amusement assaulted the chamber, reverberating in a maddening symphony of unhinged glee. "Of course you don't! It's always more fun to find out what it is after it's already been forced inside you!" It taunted me with bitter contempt, relishing its twisted game as it moved in on my left arm. Its grotesque head looked up with malicious anticipation, eyes darting from the tip of the needle to my vulnerable arm to my fear-struck eyes faster than one can blink.

"Do you believe in God?" it jeered, tilting its head completely to the side, daring the laws of anatomy almost to the point of snapping its own neck. I fervently nodded my head yes, hoping this desperate plea would spare me the horror of whatever it was about to do.

"Good!" it screeched. It raised the needle into the air with one swift motion before plunging it deep into my flesh. A searing agony unleashed in my violated vein. The creature sneered, revealing serrated teeth that were sharp as knives.

Instantly I felt a corrosive fire cascade through my veins as the fluid burned its way toward the void that once held my heart. I began to waver in and out of consciousness, held by a fragile thread of awareness.

I looked to my left at the tray on which the ghastly boxes of my entrails lay. My gaze fixated, fighting through the blur to decipher the label on one of the ominous boxes. *Heart.* It started to pulsate. With each passing second, the beat intensified as a primal drumming, reaching for me in a rhythmic frenzy. The tray could not contain its attempts to flee. The box bounced urgently, a tintinnabulation on the tray and cart, then vaulted from its confines and smashed onto the floor. The impact echoed, causing an ear-splitting cyclone of sound around the round room. On impact, the box split, sending my heart sliding across the floor.

In perverse delight, the shadow split, becoming a ghastly visage of two ravenous creatures, reeking of death and flush with fury. They lunged at my heart as I watched helplessly, impotent to respond, still bound to the chair, unable to wake from the nightmare's grip. They devoured my organ, screaming in savage delight as I screamed in pain.

Crimson blood gushed from my chest.

Then, the agony of my vision dissolved to black.

I jolted up, out of my sleep, drenched, sweating, and shaking. I grabbed my chest, searching for my pulse.

Thump, thump. Thump, thump. It was there. My precious heart intact.

Slowly, my breath returned to a stabilized rhythm. I looked around the bus. Everyone but me and the driver were asleep. I rose and walked to the bathroom at the back of the bus. I splashed water on my face. *What the hell did that mean? It was just a bad dream.*

A gnawing unease persisted. I was out of the dream, but standing at the entrance to a labyrinth of cryptic questions and haunting warnings for my waking world. The faucet's water offered no solace; the streaks in the bathroom mirror remained. *It was just a bad dream.*

Breathe. I can find comfort, even from a stranger.

Breathe. Obsessing over what I look like does not reflect what I am inside.

Breathe. Beware of thinking I am free rather than knowing I am free.

Breathe. I will keep moving forward.

9

Oklahoma City

Breathe. When you pause for just a moment, an opportunity will present itself.

Breathe. If you are lost in the chaos of thoughts and feelings, you can touch the physical world and become grounded.

Breathe. Knowing where you are, compared to where you started, will provide a sense of calm.

Breathe. Keep moving forward.

The night had passed. We had been traveling throughout its restless hours. Sleep, when it had come, had not been easy, given the lingering torment of my dream. My most recent waking was to wide fields scattered with wind turbines and the unpleasant chatter of the bus driver's wife. Her middle-aged face was capped with blonde hair whose roots had not been touched up in a while. She reminded me too much of what I could remember of Berna. Her voice, the gravelly way she spoke from a lifetime of cigarettes, her energy, her posture—it all seemed off. I was not fond of her.

The bus made its way onto the exit that would lead to downtown Oklahoma City's Greyhound Bus Station. Tammy had written down her number for me on a scrap of paper.

"Call me when you want to come and see me!" she said hopefully. Tulsa was the next city over, so the possibility seemed real. I waved goodbye as she hopped onto the next bus.

Once again, I found myself alone in yet another stinky bus station. Rather than thoughts, at this moment it was my physical senses that demanded attention. I could smell myself. I desperately needed to shower. I looked for a restroom. A sign pointed to the back of the station and up a flight of stairs. The men's room had multiple stalls but no showers. I entered one of the stalls and locked myself in, taking a moment to think. I sat on the toilet and pondered how I could clean myself without making a scene and without being walked in on in the open layout.

A plan formed. It would not be ideal. I was embarrassed, but this was all I could think to do. Foot traffic in the bathroom was consistent; modesty and avoidance of entrants were impossible. I went to the sink and got a miniature cup that was provided for water. After filling it up with hand soap from the sink, I went back to the stall. I started to strip naked behind the closed metal door. The pipes for the toilet emerged directly from the wall, so there was no tank.

I could not believe that it had come to this point and that I was going to do what I was about to do, but with the way I smelled, I had to do something. There in the bowl was the toilet water. I was going to have to bathe myself in it. Absolutely disgusted, I flushed the toilet to assure myself that the water was fresh. After only minor hesitation, I dunked my hands into the water and splashed myself with it. There was no hesitation in slathering the soap all over my body. I scrubbed profusely, simultaneously trying not to make too much noise. I hated myself in that moment. But I didn't consider going home.

How did I go, in a matter of days, from not having to worry about money, with a family who provided for all of my needs, with (by outside standards) a good life with family and friends, to being a sixteen-year-old runaway boy? *Why the hell did I choose to be homeless?* Somewhat rational questions thrashed through my head in quick succession, warded off just as quickly by somewhat irrational retorts. *I am free to do whatever I want. No one can tell me what to do. I will find a man to take care of me. I will finally be able to express myself sexually, exactly as I desire, without any shame or judgment.*

I finished drying myself with a mound of paper towels before putting my clothes back on. Now "clean", I grabbed my things and headed out of the station. I had never been to Oklahoma City and I had no idea where I was to go. My gut pointed me in the direction of downtown. It was around three o'clock when I decided to visit the library. I stopped the next person to cross my path and was pointed in the direction of the nearest library, just three blocks away. Perfect!

When I arrived I headed upstairs to the computer lab. I sat for a second, conjuring imaginary emails from my parents, thinking about all the things they would say, relishing that they might beg me to come back. I had the emotional upper hand. Once I knew they were looking for me, I would leave them wanting, with no answers and no contact. Then I had a flickering moment of doubt, masquerading as a justifiable defense for my anger: *if* they even bothered to email me.

I proceeded to log in and navigated straight to my email. Nothing. I checked my Myspace account. Again there was nothing. This made me so angry. *They aren't even looking for me!* I had been right to doubt them. I knew they did not love me!

Then an avenue of salvation for my manipulative mental war emerged. I went to Google and typed "missing children from Montana." *Maybe, maybe . . .* I wanted to see if anyone had reported me. Still nothing?

I felt defeated, my hope for emotional victory had failed. This hurt. I was hurt. *How could my parents not even report me missing?*

Then I saw it, my given name, Bruce Wayne Brackett. The victory I thought I would celebrate did not materialize. Instead, quite surprisingly, I was mortified. I had done this to myself. Apparently I wanted their love. I think I even knew they loved me, but I didn't feel worthy of it. If Berna, the woman who birthed us, had so easily dismissed us, we obviously weren't worthy of anyone else's love. That belief had transformed into the anger that had caused me to slowly fall apart.

I logged off the computer and went back downstairs, dejected. At the front desk I asked for a map of the city, unsure of what to do next. The man offered some suggestions, recommending I go to an area called Bricktown, where I would find a movie theatre, restaurants, and several clubs.

I found myself in line at the movie theatre, wanting to get my mind off things. Being the true gay boy that I was, the decision of movies was an easy one. I went to see *Hairspray*! I made my way to the safety and comfort of the back row. I shuffled into my seat and just relaxed for what felt like the first time since this misadventure had begun. When the last of the credits had rolled, I found myself in a singsong type of mood. I felt good. I felt safe. I had become so lost in the movie that the thought of where I was going to sleep that night had scarcely crossed my mind. *A park?* Only homeless people did that. Then reality struck: I was a homeless person. I reminded myself that just hours before I had bathed in a toilet bowl.

However, if it was going to be a park, I knew which one. The beautiful park with lush lawns, manicured gardens, and fountains just down the street next to the bus station. Walking there was an exercise in trepidation and determination. I found a spot under a cluster of bushes by a large cascading waterfall. I pulled a bundle of clothes from my duffel and swaddled them to create a pillow. I lay down and stared into the sky.

Time battered on. Restlessly, I flipped from side to side, unable to manage even an approximation of comfort. My irritation grew until the only option was to stand and scream. There was no warning; the errant emotions came out of nowhere. One second I was crying, then the next I was laughing hysterically. Rage struck me like lightning. Things weren't working like I had imagined. I didn't feel safe. I had nowhere to go. I felt hopeless. It was horrible. I started to pace, faster and faster, insidious panic moving my feet. I began to cry once more. This time the words came out.

"I want to go home!" I sobbed repeatedly. "I want to go home!" The park was no use, it offered no shelter from my tormented thoughts. I began to walk the streets, alone. "What the hell is wrong with me? *Why am I crazy!?*" I wept softly, crying to myself.

Having been diagnosed with bipolar disorder at 11, I had tried many meds and none had worked. I wasn't on meds now. The worst part about it was that, sometimes, I knew I was in desperate need of help. However, I could only grasp reality for a few moments before snapping back into a disastrous autopilot once more, a rag doll tossed about by my mental state.

After several hours of trudging the streets, crying myself into exhaustion, I finally came to a crashing stop. With no juice left, I fell asleep under a bush by a bench in the same park, but on the other end. Pointless circles. Futile running.

I awoke to voices . . . not in my head. After my eyes had adjusted, I could make out two women about 30 feet away. They were looking in my direction and talking in hushed tones to each other. When they detected my waking, they quickly turned and walked the other way.

"Stupid bitches! They got nothing better to do than to stop and stare at the homeless boy on the streets. Get a life!" I snarled, missing the irony of telling them to get a life.

The humidity was climbing, the temperature rising. The putrid smell of garbage saturated the air. I was becoming uncomfortable in the heat and wanted to find an air-conditioned building. I decided to go back to the public library, but it was still closed. I sat, leaning myself against a fountain not far from the entrance.

I noticed my feet. They were really dirty. I took off my shoes and dipped my feet into the water. Chills shot through my body and goosebumps formed on my skin as my feet glided through the frigid water. Easily amused, I wiggled my toes and chuckled to myself. It is amazing how soothing something as simple as water can be. Just the feeling of it sloshing around my feet and squirting between my toes was therapeutic. Its elemental caress grounded me in the present. I forgot about the world of thoughts and feelings and enjoyed the physical one. The subtle hum of the city awakening dissolved into a comforting sonic surround. The clean lines of the gleaming modern library blurred into an impressionist background for this simple pleasure. I had forgotten that I was a runaway boy and had completely surrendered to the moment. The digital clock across the street finally turned to read 9:00 a.m. It was no longer just the air conditioning that I craved, and unlike my usual need for a computer, this visit wasn't about porn. I needed to get back onto a computer to see if there was any word from my family or friends. I also started to think about other cities I could go to. The gay nightlife I had hoped for was not to be found in downtown Oklahoma City. Maybe Chicago, I thought. Just the name Chicago got me excited!

When the library's glass doors slid open, I yanked my feet out of the fountain, grabbed my footwear, and raced inside. Once again I went to my Myspace profile and saw that I had no new messages. *What the hell?! Why is nobody reaching out to me? They know I'm gone but they aren't going to contact me? Screw them!* I thought. *If they can move on without me, then so can I.*

Chicago it was, the obvious solution to all my woes. Just as quickly as I had entered the library, I grabbed my bag and left, headed for the

Greyhound station. I had just $140 left and hoped that this would be enough to get me to Chicago. There it would be easy to find a gay area of town and sell myself for money or shelter. Here it was—one of those fleeting moments of coherence: *what a messed-up way of thinking,* I thought to myself. And just like that, it was gone.

The time it took me to race the three blocks' distance was as if they didn't even exist. Practically at the moment the decision had occurred, I was through the smelly waiting area and at the desk asking the cost of a ticket for the next bus to Chicago. The man's reply stalled my charge. I was $10 short.

I quickly shifted plans. I could try Dallas, which was closer, I must have enough money to get there. The man sold me the ticket, not questioning the dramatic and sudden change of plan; as I'd found at the previous bus stations, he couldn't care less.

The hunger that had developed from many hours of activity and many hours without sustenance allowed me to forgo my budding body dysmorphia and order a hamburger and a Diet Coke. My stomach was aching from more than a day without food. The smell of the meat cooking exaggerated my cravings. It took mere seconds to dispatch the delicious hamburger. I could have eaten three more and I wanted to. Thoughts of my quickly vanishing money halted my ravenous instincts. I was running very low. *I'll just get something along the way to Dallas or when I get there.*

The expression on my face may have summoned the pity of a red-headed woman and little boy who approached me. Perhaps her motive was to cheer me up; more likely they just needed a seat. "May we sit with you? Every other seat is taken," she asked hopefully.

"Of course. I won't be here long." I replied, instinctively forming a smile on my face.

"You don't mind if we pray, do you?" she asked.

"No, not at all," I said. Pray? Pray to whom and for what, I wondered. After they had finished their prayer, they started to eat.

I feigned interest. "So where are you two traveling to?" I inquired.

"Home, Chicago," the woman replied with a smile.

Son of a bitch! Of course she would be from the place I so badly wanted to go. Ten dollars short! "Oh, that's nice!" I proclaimed with a very fake, enthusiastic smile. From that point, the conversation revolved around how fabulous Chicago was. I remember we ended up talking about a neighborhood called Boystown, which was known as one of the gayest areas in the country. It sounded amazing! All I needed was the money. It was going to be the next place I went. But tonight, my destination was Dallas.

I thanked them for the conversation and headed to Bricktown to watch the tourists.

Luck preceded me. After a brief attempt at panhandling, I found some coins abandoned on the street. It wasn't ten dollars, but my coffers were a few coins heavier.

Breathe. When I pause for just a moment, an opportunity will present itself.

Breathe. If I am lost in the chaos of thoughts and feelings, I can touch the physical world and become grounded.

Breathe. Knowing where I am, compared to where I started, will provide a sense of calm.

Breathe. I can and will keep moving forward.

10 | Angels in Dallas

> Breathe. Not everything is as you see it, and that's okay.
>
> Breathe. Even when you don't ask for help, help is usually provided. You just have to be willing to accept it.
>
> Breathe. When fire strikes, remove yourself from the flames before you get hurt.
>
> Breathe. Keep moving forward.

What was Dallas going to be like? I wondered. I had never been to Texas and was growing excited. I stood in line to get on the bus. Not many people were boarding, maybe 20. *Good! I'll be able to get a good seat.*

The quiet of the bus was unexpected and complete. Nobody was talking. Everyone had their own space: a bus full of solo souls, no one traveling with anyone else. Even the driver had a distant look, looking out over the distances.

I turned on my overhead light, pulled out my journal, and started to write. *Here I am again, sitting on a Greyhound bus headed towards god only knows where . . . it has been 3 days since I have spoken with anybody I know. So far, I am still alive, so I must be doing something right.*

I thought about what I wrote. *So far I am still alive.* I lost awareness of time and fell asleep to the sound of the diesel engine roaring stridently in the back.

Hours later, I awoke as the bus was pulling into the downtown Dallas station. I pulled my bag over my shoulder, hopped off the bus, and walked with false determination through the station, down a long hallway, and out a set of glass doors.

Time continued to pass without measure. I was in a fog. Several blocks of aimless wandering may have taken minutes or hours. I happened upon a deserted park away from the downtown throngs and hopped over its ineffective retaining wall. I sat for a moment, then I opened my bag and pulled out a blue blanket I had bought at a Goodwill in Bozeman. After laying it out on the grass, I tried to make myself as comfortable as possible. It was the middle of July, so the weather was uncomfortably hot and humid, even in the middle of the night.

I started to rummage through my bag. Finding my roll of money, I pulled it out, took the rubber band off, and began to count. I sat there and counted it over and over, each time becoming increasingly panicked, each time hoping the number I came to was wrong. Even with the change I found in Bricktown, I had less than ten dollars.

My focus became myopic. I was so fixated on my fast-fading money that I neglected my surroundings. Quite unexpectedly, a large man moved into my space. Startled, I stuffed the money back in my bag and quickly stood up to face him. He remained motionless. No words, no movement, just looking. The scant light of the street lights seemed far away.

There was a radiance about him, but his features were nebulous in the dark. He was a Black man, about six feet tall and roughly two hundred pounds, and he wore loose black clothes. What I couldn't see, I could feel. His presence was intense; I could sense the potential of his power and felt unsettled. It was as if he were cloaked in a celestial haze.

"Hello." The man's voice was deep and calm, with a disquieting serenity. I said nothing in reply. "Not to get all in your business, but what are you doing here so late?" the stranger questioned.

"What are *you* doing here so late?" I snapped back sarcastically.

"Yes, of course." An enigmatic chuckle followed. "I saw you over here, and I could not help but notice that you seemed to be a bit lost. What's your name?"

"Todd Klein," I stated.

Shaking his head back and forth he said steadily, "No, it's not." The calmness and certainty were not what I was expecting from him. "Sit down," he instructed with a guiding command. I did. "What's your name?" he asked again.

"Bruce," I replied.

"Good name."

He closed the short distance between us and sat down next to me, uncomfortably close, as if we were kin.

"Where are you from?"

"I live around the corner," I said trying to get him off my back, my unease at his intrusive closeness unmistakable.

"No, you don't. Where are you from?" His assertiveness and insistence on honest answers were bothersome.

"Jesus, man! What do you want?" I deflected defiantly, trying to avoid the answer.

"Do you know where you are? This is Dallas, kid. A pretty, young boy like you with rainbow bracelets is a sure scream for death in this neighborhood. You're in the wrong area with that, baby. You got to get out of here." The air of protective guardianship hit me.

"I can take care of myself, but thanks." I brushed him off.

"I'm just trying to help. You're in the wrong part of town. If you don't leave this park tonight, you won't ever leave. Do you understand me? You will die." The warning was pure. An insistent alert raised as a divine shield. This vacant park was not a refuge. The dull cement at my feet was not hallowed ground.

He had delivered his message and walked away quickly, vanishing into the seeping shadows before I had processed his protective edict.

With the echo of his words warping in the mist of my confusion, I jumped up and chased after him. "What do you mean?" I called out to him, but I could sense that this unsolicited guardian was gone. I turned the corner. There was no one to be seen. He had just vanished. The hair on the back of my neck shot up. Completely freaked out, I raced back to my bag, grabbed my things, and got the hell out of that park.

I spent the rest of the night wandering the streets, smoking what little weed I had left, and fighting to stay awake. When resistance seemed futile, I found the most sheltered area I could, a pedestrian street, free from traffic, with a dividing wall that obscured views. I climbed under a bench hoping no one would see me. It wasn't a bunk or a bunker, but it gave the illusion of cover.

Sleep coiled upon me and I began to dream. However, something was far too familiar about this dream; its opening darkness beckoned me into an oppressive déjà vu. I felt tugged forward by an invisible force, beckoning me through the pitch-black abyss that led to the corridor, which led to the door, behind which my life would be handed again to the demons and creatures of the night. Tendrils of neon green smoke escaped from across the threshold and encircled me. I was now hostage to this nocturnal terror.

I was in my nightmare again, pulled inexorably toward the door. A blunt object hit me, hurling me onto the floor. Blood oozed from my lower lip. I was back in the room where the green and black stripes swirled in a maelstrom of spinning. An invisible power yanked me upward and hurled me to a solitary chair in the center of the chamber, my throne of awaiting torment. There was the same spectral shadow and the cart with the metal tray, which was now full of needles. I tried to scream. I fought to break free. *Why can't I just wake up?!* My subconscious fought the chains of paralysis, but my body remained locked in this unwanted reverie. I commanded myself: *Try to twitch! Try to gasp! Anything to wake up!*

A door creaked open behind me. An incongruent saccharine scent cut through the humidity. All movement of the air had ceased. The oxygen leaked slowly away. The remaining gases compressed, rendering it contradictorily stifling and suffocatingly thin. Through the insidious haze, a woman emerged, unlike the phantoms. She was tangible, beautiful, inconsistent with the severe setting. Her stilettos might have been glamorous if not for the sharpness of the pointed heels. She wore a white nurse's uniform, its purity and rigidity unsettling.

"Long night?" she asked, her voice dripping with suspect compassion. Confusion gripped me. Who was she?

"I'm Jennifer. I am your nurse for the day. Are you hungry?" she asked sweetly. She was not to be trusted, her role in this wicked game was not yet certain.

I feigned agreement as my spine shuddered.

"Alright. I will feed you." Her honeyed declaration was tinged with satisfaction; a calculation had been made. She walked in the direction of the cart. The glint of the needles caused my eyes to widen and sweat to form on my brow.

"Relax. This won't hurt a bit." Calmness in her voice assured the opposite. The allure of her fairytale beauty contradicted the horrors unfolding. She reached under the cart with the deftness of a master magician. A blender materialized in her clutches before being slammed onto the cart. Her bare hands seized a handful of needles and dropped them into the blender.

She began to bleed. One of the needles had pricked her delicate flesh. Delighted, not deterred, she held her bleeding hand over the blender and allowed her ruby plasma to mix into the grisly elixir. The machine whirred to life, twisting the alarming components into an unhallowed concoction.

A mad gleam flickered in her eyes. She picked up the grotesque mixture and dumped it upon me. Needles stabbed from every angle, raining down, and plunging deep into my exposed flesh. Her eyes frosted in a demonic haze and she screeched to her comrades, "*It's time!*"

From the shadows between the stripes materialized a battalion of towering 13-feet-tall corpses. Their demented pleas resonated as shrill screams around the circular enclosure. They begged for freedom from the confines of my subconscious, their deranged desires ready to be unleased into my waking world. "Wake up! *Wake up!*" they screamed, eager for escape into my reality. Their unholy game was ready. "Come play with us!"

I woke up, and realized I was in front of the library in downtown Dallas. I looked up, still in the haze of my thoughts, and my eyes met those of a striking woman. She was about my height, petite, gorgeous, with neat black braids and perfect chocolate skin. Her flawless presentation made her age indeterminable. She was very put together, with a fitted black T-shirt, hip-hugger jeans, gleaming white sneakers, and a tote bag full of books that she was putting into the trunk of her silver Audi. Her head was tilted to hold her cell phone between her shoulder and ear. Once our eyes locked, she did not take them away. After a momentary pause she continued her conversation, never releasing her gaze. When she finished speaking, she called out to me and asked if I was okay.

I stood up and walked over to her and without any thought I blurted out, "I need your help."

"You look like you could use help," she replied, matter-of-factly, without judgment. Even in this simple exchange, she exuded effortless class.

"You have no idea. Hi, I'm Todd." My voice was desperate and heavy.

"Nice to meet you, Todd. I am Orlean. What is wrong? How can I help you?" she replied.

"Well, it's a long story." I began to spout a package of lies. I told her that my parents had kicked me out of the house because I was gay and that I had no money or food and needed shelter.

She didn't even delay, as if helping me was a forgone conclusion. "Get in. I have an idea," she announced. "I am going to take you to the LGBT youth center here in Dallas and they should be able to help you further."

We drove around for a while, stopping a few times to ask for directions trying to locate the center. It felt almost like a Sunday outing. We talked about what she did for a living and where she was from. It was evident that she was genuinely a very sweet, caring woman and wanted to help me out, but she wasn't naïve. I am certain she did not believe a word I said to her. She knew I was a runaway. As we drove on, she continued to question me about my situation. Realizing she did not believe my lies, I slowly revealed more of the truth, my real name and where I was from.

"Oh my, you do need help. You're a long way from home!" Orlean offered graciously, with a smile on her face to calm me.

Finally, we arrived at the center. She accompanied me inside. To our left was a window with a young man sitting behind a counter. His hair was styled up and he was very handsome. As we walked in, he moved his attention from his *Us Weekly* magazine to Orlean. "Hello and welcome. How may I help you?"

"Hi," replied Orlean. "Well, we have a little situation that I am not fully aware of how to deal with. This is Bruce." She motioned her hand toward me. It was easy to smile on cue because I was instantly attracted to him. What a pleasant distraction he was. Orlean recounted my lie, how my family kicked me out and that I needed shelter. My attention drifted from their conversation. Moments later, Orlean thanked the man and motioned me to follow her, so I did. We walked back outside and headed to her car.

"They are not able to help us, but they've given me a list of shelters that we can try." She relayed the update optimistically. I nodded my head in approval. We arrived at our first stop. The location terrified me. The streets were filthy and the building walls were tagged in gang signs.

"What type of shelter is this?" My disgust was obvious. Orlean took the hint, likely fearful for my safety, and continued to drive past. These past few hours with her had already forged an unexpected bond between us. The next shelter on our list was closed due to an infestation of bedbugs. Our luck was fading and my hunger was growing.

Orlean pulled out her phone and called someone. "I know!" she said excitedly.

"My girlfriend can help. Now I am going to need you to trust me on this. This next shelter is going to need your parents' permission to let you stay there. What's their phone number?" she asked. I instantly become very hot.

"What? Why?" I asked, anxious.

"Bruce, I need you to trust me. I am not going to ask them anything or say anything to them. I just want you to get enrolled in this shelter. It is provided by an LGBT-friendly church." I went along with it, trusting her despite my misgivings. My gut said no, but I gave her my parents' number.

Moments later, we were pulling up in front of the church. As Orlean talked to the minister, I went to the bathroom and, for the third time, bathed with toilet water. I was so disgusted with myself.

While leaving the stall to get paper towels I caught a glimpse of my shirtless torso in the mirror. I had lost weight. "Not good enough!" I scolded myself angrily. I pulled the skin on my stomach and on my back. I hated myself for having skin that I could pinch. After grabbing the paper towels, I got as far away from the mirror as possible. I must have lingered in the bathroom a long time, because when I got back a bag of Burger King was waiting for me in the main office.

"I went and grabbed us a bite to eat. You looked hungry," Orlean said.

"Thanks," I said with a fake smile plastered on my face. I *was* hungry, but I did not want to eat it. *So many calories.* I ate some of it just so I didn't come across as rude. I liked Orlean and didn't want to offend her.

As I finished eating, I looked up and saw a female police officer step through the office door. "Hello, Mr. Brackett," she said. Everything stopped. My heart jumped into my throat and my body became stone cold. The fondness I felt for Orlean instantly turned to hate. I knew that she had called the police. I was so angry I could not make eye contact with either of them. The only words that made their way to my mouth were "Get me out of here." I was humiliated, but part of me was relieved.

I didn't jump up. I didn't try to run. "Turnaround, son." the officer said. "You are not being arrested, we are just taking you into custody until your father can come down and get you." She handcuffed me and led me out of the office, then out of the building.

The next thing I remember clearly was screaming on the phone to my mother. "What do you care if I am okay or not? You hate me! You don't care! You even told me you would not look for me!" I was willfully ignoring that they had placed me on the missing person's list because I believed my own lies. Even now my parents don't remember why they didn't send emails or messages over social media. Perhaps they were enacting the principles of "tough love" that were in fashion, or perhaps they thought I needed to realize my folly on my own, and that any attempt to demand I stay would only push me farther away.

The officer drove me to the other side of the city to yet another shelter. This one was for children, but it looked different, more like a prison. It was a well-secured environment with few windows. The officers escorted me inside to a holding room where I waited as they rummaged through my bag looking for drugs or weapons. I had neither.

What's next? I kept thinking. Where was my life taking me? Was this my long and lonely downward spiral toward death? I was being dramatic. *I might as well be dead,* I thought. *It would be easier than doing what I'm doing now.* The officer interrupted my thoughts to lead me down a hallway and into another room, where a nondescript civil servant typed fiercely on her computer. Her attention turned to me as I sat down. She began to speak in a perfunctory monotone. The intake questions began. Are you sleeping well? Are you depressed? Are you suicidal? When was the last time you ate? And so on and so on. I answered by rote. The drill was familiar from the years of meetings with therapists and social workers.

After all the questions were asked and answered, I was given food and a hygiene kit. I brushed my teeth and took to the bed they assigned me to. It was uncomfortable, but it was my first bed in nearly a week. In the past 24 hours, a strange man had told me I would die if I did not leave the park, I was captive in a night terror, and I wandered the city with a kind stranger. It was as though I had encountered an angel, a demon, and a savior. With the feelings and memories of those encounters still fresh and vivid in my mind, I rolled over and lost myself in yet another night of restless sleep.

Breathe. Not everything is as I see it, and that's okay.

Breathe. Even when I don't ask for help, help is usually provided. I just have to be willing to accept it.

Breathe. When fire strikes, I must remove myself from the flames before I get hurt.

Breathe. I can and will keep moving forward.

11

A Flight
to Freedom

Breathe. Each failure is an opportunity for you to see your success in trying. So try again.

Breathe. What you think someone is thinking is usually the farthest thing from the truth. Stop overthinking because it only damages you.

Breathe. You can put on all the makeup and high fashion you want to make you look good. This disguise still doesn't change who you are on the inside.

Breath, and keep moving forward.

I awoke to an unsettling shout from a large man. In one swift motion, he turned on the light and ripped the blanket off of me. I was left lying on the bed in nothing but the blue scrubs that had been given to me the night before. Discombobulated yet compliant, I followed his orders to get up and get dressed.

"You're getting out of here this afternoon, kid!" he said with a smile. "Your father is coming down today to pick you up. He's coming all the way . . . from Montana?"

"Yeah, all the way from Montana," I mumbled back.

"You have an amazing dad who must love you very much for him to travel all that way to spring you out of here!" he declared, observing a truth I didn't want to acknowledge.

I responded as dully as possible, hoping to end our interaction. "Yeah, I guess."

I suspected that breakfast would consist of rubbery scrambled eggs and cardboard bacon. I was correct. This would be the first time I had seen my father since I ran away, and I was extremely nervous. Unlike breakfast, I did not know what to suspect his reaction would be upon seeing me. I had been missing for one week. I was partly relieved but also resentful that he was coming to get me. Questions started to take over my mind. *Will he hate me? Will he be happy to see me? What will he say?*

After hours of anxious waiting, my father's rental car finally pulled up. My fear was unjustified. He stood with his arms wide open, waiting for me to approach. I did embrace him, although with reluctant hesitation about whether his true thoughts were actually in line with his welcoming actions.

My dad had always tried to impart wisdom through stories. He once told me a story about a man and the three lessons he had to learn in life. The first lesson was "Always save your anger for another day."

Once you know the complete situation you are facing, it might not be worth getting angry over. This was something my father took seriously.

The second lesson was "Never meddle in anyone else's business," because it's a good way to create enemies. Keep your opinions to yourself unless someone asks you for help or advice. Part of me wished my father wouldn't meddle in my business, but I had definitely dug myself into a hole and needed help.

The last lesson was "Never leave the old road." If you find yourself facing something unfamiliar, stick with what you know best. Don't go off in a different direction than what you have mapped out for yourself because changing course makes it more likely that you will encounter something you are unprepared for. You may seek adventure and you may fail, but this is how you find lessons for the future. When I left home, I had definitely left the old road—and I had failed.

Those three lessons were in my mind as we faced each other, and they reassured me that my dad didn't hate me. I knew that he loved me, and that was enough to make all my nerves go away, for the moment. I had his support, even though I was sure he had a month's worth of lectures waiting for me.

As we drove to the airport, we were unnervingly quiet. What could be said? This space left my mind a dangerous hole to fill. The second we walked through security, my unhealthy feelings started to race back to me. I couldn't help looking at all the men throughout the terminal. I became overwhelmed with the force of desire and yearned to submit to them. My hidden wants flooded my mind and broke down any rational thought processes, dissolving my innocence and any care of safety. As we took our seats on the plane, my mind raced with thoughts of men, mixed with the idea of what would happen when I got home.

My dad broke the silence. "Are you done?" he asked me. I knew he was talking about my erratic behavior and running away.

"Yeah, I am done." I told him what he wanted to hear, lying through my teeth. I had miles left in me, hundreds of miles.

As our plane took off, we sat side by side in silence while our minds and souls screamed. My father didn't have to say a word for me to know how frustrated he was, but I couldn't appreciate in that moment that it was born of love and worry. He would go out of his way to make sure that the world was mine and that I never had to worry. I just couldn't return the favor at that point in my life. I knew that when we got home, things would be different. I was in some pretty deep shit with my parents. I lost all privileges and was officially grounded for the first time in my life. I would have to find a way to dig myself out of this hole I had jumped into.

When we got home, I stood in my wretched bedroom and felt as miserable as ever. I often felt batshit insane when the room was silent and still. That feeling was inching its way over me now. Like a towering shadow peeling from the walls, I could feel a thick air creep its way through my body like a mist of compulsion. An itching and prickling sensation mutated into a craving to indulge in dirty, real-life sexual fantasies. My past trauma was becoming my present.

I darted out of my bedroom and directly to my father's shop in the garage. He was sitting in a chair, absorbed in a project involving string. "Can I talk to you?" I blurted out, shaking. Emotions were fresh, confusing, and raw. It was all too new. I felt like shit talking to him because I felt bad for hurting him and Mom, but in an awesome and surprising moment, I had snapped back into reality and could identify that what I had done was wrong. I was "awake" and part of me wanted to stay that way.

"Yes, of course," my father replied, his voice a mixture of assurance and concern.

I hesitated. I was still unsure if I could be honest with him.

"Are you okay? What can I help with?" He was calm and measured. I could see that he was truly one hundred percent there for me, so I started to let it out.

"I need your help! I need to be saved or something," I started in, fumbling for a way to be vulnerable. "I am always so uncomfortable or overly sexual. It's almost as if I'm trapped. It's almost like I need to be trapped in a cement room and never let out until I'm fixed! What's wrong with me?" I began to panic.

My father wrapped an arm around the back of my neck and placed his hand on my shoulder to comfort me. "There is nothing wrong with you," he stated resolutely. "You are just going through a lot, and we will find the help you need and keep you safe, son. Please remember that you are loved!"

Anyone expressing their love to me made me so uncomfortable. *I don't deserve it. If only they knew what I really was.*

After speaking with my dad, I remember sulking in my bedroom, perturbed at the situation I had put myself in. All I wanted was to get out of it—and fast. *But how?* I was already in so much shit, would it matter if I got into more trouble? I had already screwed up everything for myself. Some might write it off as a teenage pity party, but I legitimately felt alone and helpless.

I sat on my bed rocking back and forth, trying to come up with a plan of escape. When no plan formed, I decided that I would play dress-up. At least that would help take my mind off of the thousands of racing thoughts. I opened my closet and started rummaging through my clothes. I picked out the most "fashion forward" things that a gay boy in Butte, Montana, could possibly have. Everything must be black, I decided. I would be wearing absolutely no color, nor anything that could resemble happiness. I donned black pin-striped Calvin Klein trousers that I had purchased at Goodwill for $3.50. They always made me feel good. Next I selected a black turtleneck that I layered with a dark tweed vest I wore very often. Accessories were essential. I started by putting on my fingerless leather gloves that had two small spikes on each cuff. To kick it up a notch, I wrapped myself in an oversized sheer scarf—the perfect touch of fabulousness. I wore it as a capelet shawl. Black patent leather shoes completed the look, of course. Must be patent leather!

After I finished dressing, I made my way to the bathroom to examine myself in the mirror. I looked like what I imagined a dandy boy of the 1920s might. I wasn't finished. I needed more. I needed makeup.

I pulled out my tackle box of stage makeup from under the bathroom vanity and started to paint my face a ghostly white. I caked on layers until I was paler than that dreadful nightmare nurse. Next I added black eyeliner, creating a smokey eye. I shadowed high-fashion death beneath my cheekbones to add definition and to make me look skinnier. *Must be skinny!* I settled for a deep violet lip color, a combination of crimson lifeblood and walking dead.

With each new layer that I painted on my face, I observed myself transforming and my mood changing. Everything about me, my very persona, changed as I became an alternate version of myself, an Emo/Goth kid sequestered and sulking in my cinder-block basement bedroom. When I was satisfied with my look, I finished it by crowning myself with a French beret, tilted downward ever so slightly over my right eye. I felt sexy and powerful. I felt mean . . . and I loved it. Again,

I was Narcissus, captivated in the mirror, staring at myself with wonder, examining the character I had just invented.

Then, like clockwork in my cycling bipolar mind, my mood switched, and I was instantaneously filled with anger that my body couldn't contain. Looking sharply to the left, I lasered in on the first thing I could rip apart. The bookshelf contained my target. There lay an unsuspecting stack of CDs. I seized as many as I could clamp my talons upon, and hurdled them across my room. They cracked and shattered against the unforgiving coldness of the cinder-block wall. Shards ricocheted everywhere.

That felt good. Do it again! I immediately grabbed the next thing I could destroy. Pictures, books, little figurines of the Statue of Liberty that I loved. In needless succession, I destroyed them all. I ripped up clothes and threw anything that I could lift or that was breakable, while grunting and letting out visceral yells of frustration and anger.

The immediacy of my fury was shocking. I wanted to break everything and anything that my parents had given me with an intention of love behind it. *I do not want to be loved, damn it!* I wanted out of my life . . . and away from everything good. I wanted to be dark and dangerous. I was seduced by the illusion of living the life of some houseboy whore. My split mind looked for a false salvation. I can find relief under the care of a rich man who will only use me and abuse me for his most pleasurable fantasies; I can have satisfaction without love. The distortions of my thoughts flashed a neon green. *That's what I will be good at . . . so why not just do that?! Run . . . .*

I was sucked out of my delusion and back into reality by a sudden, intent pounding on my bedroom door. My heart skipped a beat. I ceased creating havoc in my bedroom and froze, staring at the door. My mother's voice came from behind it.

"Bruce are you okay? I am very worried! I just want to make sure you're okay! Open this door!" she demanded.

I wish she would just die. Disappear and never return. This woman is going to be the death of me.

I waited. I said nothing.

This time she raised her voice. "Bruce, open this door!"

My response was delivered plainly and clear, in a low monotone. "Go. Away."

"This is *my* house. I bought it. Now *open* this door or we will break it down!"

I unlocked the door harshly and flung it open forcefully, revealing to her the dark monster I had become.

Her response was unexpected. "Well, I got to give it to you, Bruce. You look as sad as you feel, and you still do it in style." A cockeyed smile graced her face. "At least you look good doing it." She looked around my room, taking in the devastation before continuing. "I'm sorry you are in so much pain. You will need to clean this up, though." Her command was nonchalant, but her next statement seemed sincere, and practiced. "Remember you are loved." With that, she turned around and headed up the stairs.

I waited until she was completely out of sight before I closed and relocked the door. I wanted to be a thousand miles away from this life. I wanted to be living my *own* life. *Run. . . .*

I paused again in front of my mirror, gazing into the emptiness of my eyes. *Go. . . . Run. . . . You will be free.* Like clockwork, my mood changed again. And at the same moment, so did my plan.

I cleaned up my room, enough to clear my thoughts, then I grabbed a big duffel bag and left it open on the bed. Once again, I packed the hope of a new life into it, this time with items I would really need. This time I *wasn't* coming back.

In the middle of the night, I stole the keys to my mom's Lexus and walked out the front door. Between the $200 I had and the $200 in change my mom kept in the trunk for the candy shop, I was set. *Four hundred is enough until I get to where I'm going.* Where was I going? *I don't care. Just go fast!* I plopped myself behind the wheel and sat in absolute stillness. Silence. The next choice was entirely mine. *Okay, hot shot, where to?* In a surprising instance of coherence, I put the car into neutral and let it slide down the hill and away from the house before I turned the car on. I didn't want to wake a soul. I was possessed by an energy that matched the darkness I slipped away in. I was beckoned onward. *Come play with us.* I drove off, never looking back.

Breathe. Each failure is an opportunity for me to see my success in trying, so I will try again.

Breathe. What I think someone is thinking is usually the farthest thing from the truth. I will stop overthinking because it only damages me.

Breathe. I can put on all the makeup and high fashion I want to make me look good. This disguise still doesn't change who I am on the inside.

Breath, and keep moving forward.

12

Boystown

Breathe. If you are smart enough to get yourself into a situation, you are smart enough to get yourself out.

Breathe. You are only hurting yourself when you give in to someone who doesn't have your true better interest in mind. Let them go and move on without them.

Breathe. It doesn't matter how drunk or high you get. It will never make you feel better—never.

Breathe, and keep moving forward.

I drove 85 miles, across a mountain pass, to Bozeman, Montana, Big Sky Country. As I arrived, the sun was just peeking up over the mountains from the east. I drove up and down countless streets, killing time, waiting for anything to open.

My first stop was the most essential. At 8 a.m. I was parked near the bank, anxiously waiting to pull into the drive-through at the first stirrings of bank workers arriving. I wouldn't be traveling with the candy shop's change, nearly $200 in coins; I needed bills. I drove up and piled the rolls of coins into the window tray on the side of the bank. The bank teller graciously received them. *This bitch has no idea that this is a stolen car.* A sense of power rose through me. *Or that all this money I just gave her is also stolen.* Her first task of the day was an easy one. She gave me my cash and receipt and I sped away.

What next? Several hours passed as I sat in the car in the public library's parking lot. My cover was gone, my crime exposed to the growing sunlight. Unsure what was next, I continued to wait, trying to come up with a plan. My hands were still firmly gripping the steering wheel. I stared straight ahead and pondered.

I want to be in a city. A big city, where there are lots of people like me. People who feel sexual, like me. I remembered hearing about a "gay village" in Chicago called Boystown. *Perfect,* I thought. Chicago was only a two-and-a-half-day bus ride from Bozeman. I could get there in no time. The promise of the energy I craved, the rush I could already feel, was calling me. *Come play with us.*

I abandoned the stolen car. Two days and a few musky Greyhound stations later, I was dropped in the heart of the downtown Loop. To reassure myself, I kept repeating, like a mantra. *This will be everything I've wanted.*

Boystown was a few miles north, and I would be walking if I wanted to get there. With no other choice, I began my walk north, tracing the edge of Lake Michigan so I wouldn't get lost.

It was unclear what time it was, but I guessed it to be around 6:30 a.m. The streets were still desolate and shiny from a fresh rain. I was in this for good, so I didn't feel the need to rush. I ambled, indulging whatever caught my curiosity along the way. As I wandered, I noticed the increasing bustle as the people of Chicago emerged from their homes and started to go about their lives in the city.

The walk took several hours, but it delivered me to the heart of the gayest place I had ever been in my life. Boystown *was* exactly what I had hoped it to be. Rainbows waved at me from every corner: wrapped around the poles of the streetlamps, painted in the crosswalks, and upon the beautiful men who lived and worked there. It was heaven.

I made it here; now what? I walked up and down Halsted Street for a length of time that felt far longer than what it actually was. I peered through windows of the shops yet to open for the day. The new sights and sounds consumed my morning, keeping anxiety at bay.

It wasn't until midday, my third day gone, that I started to feel a little panicky. *Shit, seriously! Where will I sleep? A Shelter? How will I make this work?* Pondering my dilemma, I made my way into the public restroom at Whole Foods. Like a shadow hidden behind a wall, the demise of my future was just out of view, lurking on the other side of a bathroom stall. As I emerged from my stall and looked up, I saw him. The lights of the bathroom were harsh, so white they almost appeared green. They illuminated a tall, pale, middle-aged white man with shaggy dark brown hair. He was washing his hands in the sink and gazing at himself in the mirror. He had beautiful features. His cheekbones and jawline were defined and strong. His piercing, crystal-clear blue eyes were framed with elongated lashes that made his eyes shine brighter than they should, in an almost otherworldly way. He looked to be in pretty good shape, with back muscles that rippled through his shirt. My eyes moved down his broad back and narrow waist. He was beautiful.

My eyes traced upward, coming to rest on his face in the mirror. Chills flooded my body as our eyes met. He was looking at me looking at him. I darted my eyes away and quickly moved to the next available bathroom sink to wash my hands while trying to keep him in focus from my peripheral vision. I pretended to focus on washing my hands while continuing my furtive observation.

He finished washing and made his way past me to dry his hands. As he passed, he brushed along side of me, knocking me off balance. I couldn't tell if this was intentional.

"Sorry, kid." His voice surprised me. It was a much softer voice than what I anticipated. He winked at me, revealing the cutest smirk. If I was unsure before, I knew now. My heart jumped and landed in my stomach. It was not love at first sight but most definitely lust. He nodded his head toward the door and winked again. *Was he seriously asking me to follow him? Could this have been any easier?* For some reason, I suddenly felt shy. Although it was exactly what I was looking for, my limited real-life experience didn't provide me with the confidence to flirt back. I shuffled my feet and looked at the floor, putting my hands in my pockets. After a moment of hesitation, I looked back at him. He shrugged his shoulders and turned to walk out the door. *I need a place to stay. . . .*

"Wait!" I called out. I quickly dried my hands and rushed to follow him out of the bathroom.

His smooth talk began, "Sorry, I need to pay more attention to where I'm going, I guess. I'm Mike." I hadn't imagined it. This was an acknowledgment. He had indeed brushed alongside me and grazed my butt with the back of his hand.

"It's okay." I squeaked; my teen age outed. I cleared my throat and continued. "I mean, don't worry about it. Hi, I'm Todd."

"Where are you off to, Todd?" he asked, a hopeful sparkle in his eye.

"Nowhere good." I replied. "Just kinda hanging out."

"Hanging out? It's 9:30 in the morning. Kinda early, don't you think?" He chuckled at me. I was being played, but willingly. Mike had an empty Whole Foods shopping bag, so it was safe to assume that he was about to go shopping.

"Shopping?" I asked. "Need help?" Food and shelter. I needed both.

Mike's list was short. But we got to know some basic details about each other as he gathered Gatorades, yogurts, snack bars, and a collection of energy drinks. He was 36 and unemployed. According to his explanation, his boyfriend was rich and he didn't need to work. He also told me that I was really cute, which fed my growing infatuation, making me gush over him even more. He didn't seem to mind when I told him I was 16. In fact, he smiled.

We departed the store and continued walking down a side street, just off of Halsted in the midst of Boystown. He stared at me, looking deep into my eyes. Becoming uncomfortable, I started to shuffle my feet again.

Victimizers twist. Victims sometimes lead. Many pursue contorted needs in ways that use each other. "Any chance I could continue hanging out with you?" I asked sheepishly.

He set his bags of groceries on the ground and grabbed my shoulders. Before I knew what was happening, he planted his lips against mine. A rush went through me. We kissed for a moment and then he added, "I'd like that . . . and so would my boyfriend." *His boyfriend too? Fun!* I thought to myself.

"Aw, you are such a good boy!" he continued. His aura felt intoxicating. The words he spoke were smooth and his motions were fluid. *He seems to really like me . . . this could be it. All I have to do is to be a "good boy" and he will take care of me.*

Mike took care of me alright—if you can call feeding me meth, scarcely any food, and copious amounts of drug-fueled sex "taking care of me." This was my first encounter with hard-core drugs and my first (initially) consensual sexual experience, which brought the illusion of euphoria. However, what I had fantasized would be fun quickly turned dangerous when more men got involved. No longer were the activities consensual. My intense though innocent desires were pounded into more instances of rape than I can count on two hands. Time dissolved into nothing. The paradox is that my virgin longings for a rich older man who would care for me and understand me had fed me directly into the grips of a predator. A single pedophile had morphed into a roomful, a wealthy prison spinning with demons all chasing their own insatiable lusts. This one charming man had summoned a wicked cohort. I was lost, chasing that first high experienced with Mike just days earlier. I got what I sought, but not what I wanted.

When the partying came to an end, Mike eventually passed out as I teetered on the edge of doing the same. I knew if I wanted to live, I would need to run . . . and fast. With what little strength and determination I had left, I found myself running away as a runaway. I was bloodied and bruised, exhausted, and coming down off of what was likely a three-day high of complete and utter hell. The former me had been obliterated. I grabbed what I could find that belonged to me and left, with Mike unconscious nearby.

The realization of my fantasy was in no way a real-life fantasy. I started walking up Halstead Street and found myself back in front of the Whole Foods where I had met Mike. The LGBT Community Center was just above it. Still in a stupor, I went up and turned myself in. Not as a runaway, of course, but as an abandoned teen from London. I employed my acting skills and took on an accent and a character. The story would be that my parents abandoned me because I was gay. Lies!

The counselors at the center listened to my story and asked me a series of questions, trying to figure out exactly what to do with me. Time dilated as I started to come off the drugs. After much hunting, the counselor was able to find a bed for me in a children's shelter somewhere on the South Side of Chicago. But before they could take me in, a doctor would have to give me a physical so I could be evaluated. What I remember next is practically passing out on the examination table, from withdrawal and exhaustion. It was after midnight before I was finally on the way to the shelter, where I could get some solid, desperately needed sleep.

By pretending to be an abandoned teen from London, I had set snares for myself, but I would have to follow through with these lies for as long as possible. I feared if my true identity came out I wouldn't be in the shelter long and would possibly be sent home.

That first week at the shelter included a smattering of activities. One day the handful of children and counselors had a mini-fair in the courtyard, complete with a small bouncy house and a dunk-the-dummy, and my favorite, chocolate milk. Chocolate milk became my comfort while I was there, something familiar and simple and innocent that I latched onto. Chocolate milk was not complicated, and it could be enjoyed. Later in the week we were taken to a larger outdoor fair, with a corn maze and a bigger bouncy house, and lots of games and activities.

As the week was coming to a close at the shelter, I could feel something was about to give. One of the staff members came into my room announcing, "You will need to shower before we leave tomorrow for court."

"Court?" I questioned.

"Yeah, I guess this nice gay couple heard about your case and they want to come and meet you. Possibility of adoption? . . . I'm not sure . . . just be up and ready by 8 a.m."

My heart started racing, imagining possibilities. *Well, this is exciting. Maybe I won't have to go home after all.*

The next morning, I awoke at 7, showered as instructed, and waited for one of the staff members to go through a closet where they kept an assortment of court-appropriate outfits. After finding something that would fit me, we headed downstairs and got into a car that took us to a downtown courthouse. As we arrived, I marveled at the height of the building. I remember getting out of the car and just staring up at its imposing size for several seconds. Then the nerves started to hit. We entered the building and walked through a vast modern lobby. I could hear the echoing murmurs and percussive rhythm of feet beating against the reflective surfaces, conversations swirling all around. We made our way to the elevator bank and headed up the dizzying captive heights to the 12th floor to await my fate.

It took some time before a Child Protective Services employee checked us in. Eventually, a lovely young blonde woman came out of the wooden double doors beside the front desk. She approached me kindly.

"Hi. Todd, is it?" she asked.

"Yeah," I replied shyly, trying to maintain the British accent I had mastered during *Oliver!*

She mentioned her name, but I honestly don't remember what it was. We will just call her Katie.

"I am Katie, I will be representing you in your case." she said with a warm and welcoming smile. "I understand that you are from London." She brightened with excitement and curiosity. "I have never been to London."

"It's alright," I lied, trying to feign nonchalance, and hoping she would move on. I had never been there either.

"So," she began, "you have been through quite the rough past few weeks, I understand. Can you tell me about what has happened to you and why you are here?"

"Umm, sure. Well, not much to say really. My parents abandoned me because I came out as gay." Another lie. I was very good at lying. I was even better at acting.

"That is very horrible, I am so sorry to hear this, Todd." Katie had a sincere, sad expression on her face. "We are going to get you the help you need. Can you tell me how to reach your parents?"

"No," I stated sharply. "I don't want to go back to them. They hate me."

"I understand. That's okay. We will be able to figure this situation out for you." She changed the subject. "In the meantime, can you tell me about London? Where are you from exactly?"

I pulled a random answer out of thin air. "Woolworth Street near Union Square." It was partially true. I was from Woolworth Street. Just in Montana, not in London.

"Do you have tall skyscrapers there?" she questioned.

"Not really. I mean . . . yes. But not like what you have here in Chicago." I replied, again not having the slightest clue.

"What's your favorite part of London?" I started to become nervous, realizing that she was interrogating me. Then she came to her final question, "Do you like the Eye?" she asked with even more curiosity.

"The Eye," I replied. The contortion of my face must have read as confusion. I tried to hide my expression's betrayal and endeavored to regain my confidence. "Oh yeah, it's alright."

"Is it big?" she pushed further.

"Not really."

"Have you ever been on it?"

"Ummm . . . I have been around the area."

She paused for the briefest of moments. I was ensnared in her trap. "I was just curious, I have always wanted to go. Thank you for answering my questions. You sit tight here, and I will be right back." With that she took her clipboard, got up, and walked back through the double wooden doors.

I sat there sweating. *Did I do it? Did I fool her? Does she believe me?* After about 10 minutes, the doors reopened. This time she entered with another lawyer. At this point, my heart started beating through my chest. It was obvious. *They know.*

I don't remember exactly how the conversation went from that point forward, but they confronted me with my lying. Katie explained that the Eye was one of the most famous landmarks and tourist attractions in London. She pointed out the flaws in my story quite simply, "If you really were from London, you would know what it was. I could tell by your answers that you had no clue. So, what's the real story?"

I gave in. I told them my parents hadn't abandoned me. I didn't reveal the whole truth, however. I was still on the run and didn't want to go home.

"I was not abandoned and my name isn't Todd Klein. My name is Bruce Brackett. I am 16 years old and I am running away from a man named Bob Von Baron. He is a scary man who forced me into a prostitution ring." I continued embellishing my story, hoping to add credence to my deception. "I was just so scared to say anything because I don't want him finding me. Which is why I gave you an alias." I rambled on, trying to summon fake emotion to illicit sympathetic acceptance of my tale.

Their expressions made clear that they didn't believe me. "Oh, that is terrible. I am sure he won't find you. We will make sure of that. But we do need to know where you're truly from and who your parents are. I'm sure they're worried sick about you."

"I am from Butte, Montana, and my parents' name are Glenn and Christine."

It was obvious that there was no point in trying to avoid providing additional information. I gave them the contact information and they promptly departed through the wooden double doors. The CPS worker stayed close by my side, making sure I didn't take off. They returned shortly thereafter with orders for the CPS worker. I was out of earshot so I couldn't hear exactly what they were saying or what the plan was. I simply saw Katie glancing my way every few seconds, and sometimes gesturing toward me.

My court appearance was canceled, and we left the office building heading back to the car. The CPS worker filled me in on the updates. "A worker from the Department of Child Family Services will come and pick you up tomorrow. They are scheduling a flight home for you today. Your DCFS worker will escort you home." I went numb. I didn't want to go home yet. I wasn't done.

That night seemed endless. I tossed and turned, hardly sleeping. The next morning came as soon as my eyes finally stayed shut. I again packed my few belongings, then got into a car with the DCFS worker for the drive to Chicago's O'Hare International Airport.

"Are you actually flying with me?" I asked.

"Oh yes. I am making sure you get home," the woman replied.

The first flight departed and then landed in Salt Lake City, where we had a connection. As the connecting flight started to board, we made our way up to the gate agent collecting tickets at the entrance to a shared outdoor walkway that served many outdoor gates. The DCFS worker scanned my ticket and watched me walk toward the jetway. I turned the corner and stopped, out of her view. *This is my opportunity.*

I waited about 15 minutes, pacing back and forth, trying to make up my mind. Would I get on the flight and take the chance of being arrested when I got off the plane in Butte, or would I continue on my savage runaway adventure? My mental state at the time made my predictable, unfortunate choice inevitable. The choice was certain, but whether I would succeed in it wasn't.

I slowly peeked around the corner to make sure the DCFS worker was not still waiting. I didn't see her. Squatting down, I pulled off my shirt, dove into my bag and grabbed a hoodie—a quick disguise. I walked as fast as I could through the central gate area to the main exit, making my way toward downtown Salt Lake City.

Once again, I was on my own. No one to tell me what to do, or where to go. I was left to my own devices, more confused than ever. The maelstrom of exploits and exploitation in the last few weeks left me itching for chaos, wanting for sex, and hurting for drugs.

Breathe. If I am smart enough to get myself into a situation, I am smart enough to get myself out.

Breathe. I am only hurting myself when I give in to someone who doesn't have my true best interest in mind. I'll let them go and move on without them.

Breathe. It doesn't matter how drunk or high I get. It will never make me feel better—never.

Breathe, and keep moving forward.

13 | Salt Lake City

Breathe. Taking advantage of someone not only hurts them but weakens your potential.

Breathe. There is only one outcome for lying: getting caught. You can lie yourself silly, but one day the truth will come out and when it does, you will realize lying is never worth it.

Breathe. You can run and run and run, but you will never be able to hide from yourself.

Downtown Salt Lake was growing quiet as the workday ended. I walked around for hours, passing the famous Mormon Temple, walking up and down the streets, reaching for my purpose. Such a lofty decision was not made that evening, but a simpler one was: I would drop the British persona but keep my fake name, Todd Klein. I knew I needed to find the gay area or a gay club if I had any hope of going home with someone to fulfill my need for shelter, my lingering desire for sex, and my newfound craving for drugs.

I could get to the library to use their computers and find anything I needed, but by the time I got there it had already closed. There was a huge lawn and fountain out front, with many park benches. I walked to the top of a hill and sat down. In a now familiar ritual, I opened my bag and went through all of my belongings. *I will find what I need tomorrow when the library opens. Tonight I just need to get through the night.*

I sat. Darkness arrived and the park lights came on. The energy surrounding the library shifted from the feeling of a loving and safe environment of learning to the lonely and dangerous haunt of night walkers and homeless people. I was now one of them. Over the course of the next few hours, several people came to wash themselves in the fountain. *Oh, that's how they do it. Genius—much better than toilet water.*

I assumed it was nearing midnight when I noticed a group of people making their way up the little hill and coming in my direction. All of them were white, in their 20s, and dressed like hippie gypsies. By their appearance I could see that life might have been a bit harder for them, but they didn't scare me. The group congregated around a nearby bench. After a few minutes of watching me, one young woman, not trying to hide her scrutiny of me, made her way over.

"Hey, are you okay?" she asked as she approached.

"Yeah, I'm okay," I replied. I wasn't worried. She didn't seem threatening in any way, so I offered more. "Just staying here until the library opens tomorrow. You got the time?"

"It's 10 p.m. Are you sure you're okay? You look sad," she observed.

"Well, to tell you the truth. I am . . . and I'm scared." Upon unexpectedly uttering my own truth, the flood gates opened, and I began to cry, telling them the entire *lie*. That I had run away from this guy named Bob, who was the leader of a prostitution ring, and that

I was seeking shelter and needed to be hidden. I also added the part where my family hated me because I was gay and that I couldn't go back home.

"You can come with us," they all agreed and introduced themselves. The girl's name was Star. The two guys with her were named Ace and Corpse. Ace had dark brown hair. He was tall and thin, with a very close resemblance to Nicholas Cage. Corpse was lanky, a scrawny blond guy with sunken cheeks, messed-up teeth, and an armor of tattoos covering his arms and neck. There was another woman with them named Alicia, whose long, wavy brown hair mimicked the curves of her slightly heavier frame. "Come on, baby, let's go home," Star urged.

We made our way down the hill together and through the park. After walking for 30 minutes, we came to the outside of a very average apartment building. Even through its cinder-block exterior, I could hear a woman on the inside, wailing at someone on the phone. If the person on the other end of the line was shopping for a new asshole, they got one. Whoever it was, she was letting them have it.

"That's Mamma," Star informed me. "She takes care of all of us. Here, wait outside. I'll go get her. We have to ask permission to bring you in."

Ace and Corpse waited with me outside.

"You're gay, huh?" Corpse asked. I nodded yes. "That's cool. I'm bi. We don't care about that shit in this group. You'll be safe with us," he added, and I believed him.

A few moments later the screen door opened, and Mamma came outside. She was a short little woman in her late 20s or early 30s, crowned with a messy bun of bright pink hair. Thick glasses magnified her eyes, and she wore a tank top that was falling haphazardly off her shoulders.

"You're Todd?" She pointed at me with a lit cigarette.

"Yeah," I replied, unsure what to make of this diminutive powerhouse.

She rushed down the stairs and came right up to me, wrapping me wildly in a hug I thought would never end. "It's okay, love. You are safe now." Star told me everything. That motherfucker isn't going to ever find you or hurt you again." Her words brimmed over with passion. "I am Mamma, and I will take care of you."

She took me inside and showed me to the living room, where there was a futon, a TV, and barely anything else. They didn't have much, but it was enough for a rotating band of six to eight nomads. That night we just sat around getting to know each other. I told them my quickly evolving cover story, expanding and deepening it with additional lies.

They shared more about themselves. "We're not really a gang, but more like family members of a group called the Juggalos. We worship ICP." To prove their allegiance to the horrorcore-rap duo Insane Clown Posse, they showed me their matching tattoos of the Little Hatchet Man. "Welcome to the Juggalos!" They collectively agreed that I was welcome to stay with them for as long as I wanted to.

"Do you smoke weed?" Ace asked.

"Hell, yeah." I said, eager to fit in with my new posse. Having smoked only from a joint and tobacco pipe before, I didn't know how to use a glass pipe like the one that Ace had just picked up.

After trying to take a hit, Ace grabbed the bowl from me and chuckled. "No, no, that's not how you do it. Here, let me show you." Ace continued, "Your thumb covers up the carb hole. While you suck in, it fills the chamber with smoke. Then you let go with your thumb and inhale. Watch." He showed me step by step, then handed the bowl back. "Make sure you hold your inhale for several seconds before you exhale."

"Why?" I asked.

"So you can get high and so you don't waste my effing weed," he laughed.

I repeated the steps carefully, doing everything he had just shown me. The instant some of the smoke entered me, I choked. Puffs of smoke escaped, emphasizing each cough of embarrassment. That was *much* different than smoking meth. It burned my throat and lungs. I drank some water as the bowl was passed around. When it found its way back to me again, I decided to try a baby puff. Each time became easier for me to inhale. The buzz took over and for the remainder of the night we sat on the futon and floor watching adult cartoons on TV, laughing stupidly at nothing. I felt *fantastic!*

Over the next few days, this was the usual routine. We would sit around and smoke, eat ramen, and watch stupid TV shows. Star brought home a few different men over the course of those days. Same with Corpse and Ace. They also brought over a few women. This apartment was the revolving door of sex, drugs, and careless abandon that I had fantasized about for so long.

But this carefree lifestyle couldn't go on forever. Mamma needed more drama than that. With me as her convenient new project, Mamma went to work. She had become worried that this Bob Von Baron I had conjured would find me. So she came up with a plan to change my alias again. "I think we need to do something drastic. What do you think about changing your hair, name, and also dressing like a girl?"

"What!?" I replied, kind of excited about it. "That's genius. He would never suspect that! Okay, let's do it."

"Great, because I already bought the hair dye!"

That night, the transformation began. After dyeing my hair in the bathroom for 40 minutes to a beautiful burgundy color, then smoking copious amounts of weed, we headed to the living room, where Mamma told me to lie on the floor. "We don't have a needle, so we are just going to do this with a pair of my stud earrings."

"Won't that hurt more?" I hesitated.

"Yes, but we will first numb your ears with ice," she countered. "Now lie down."

I did as I was told and waited for the moment of pure pain to arrive. They held ice to my earlobes, but not long enough. Ace did the honors. There was no hesitation in his eagerness to be the piercer, but I was not looking forward to this. He put his knee on my chest to hold me down, then firmly pushed one earring through my ear. *Pop, pop!* The first one was in. My ears were consumed with fire. He moved on to the next one. Again, *Pop, pop!* They were both in. My ears hurt for the next week.

With the basics of my physical transformation complete, it was time for my christening. "Now, to decide on a name for you. Hmmm. . ." Mamma considered.

"I like Robbin," offered Star.

"What about Alyssa?" Alicia contributed.

"I like Angel," I said.

"*Angel!*" Mamma shouted. "That's it! Perfect. From now on you will be called Angel!"

For the next week, we went to drum circles in the park by the library, smoked ourselves into the clouds, and continued in an endless swirling cycle of living the bohemian lifestyle. I was quickly falling in love with its cyclic and predictable pleasures.

As the days passed, Mamma introduced me to more of her Juggalo family members who lived in different parts of Salt Lake. One of them was named Brandon. He was truly beautiful: tall, muscular, with the biggest bubble butt I had ever seen on a white guy. My crush on him was instantaneous. I hoped to see him more.

There were other tasks that rotated into our routine. We would go to food pantries to stock up on food and beverages. From time to time we hung out at a homeless shelter that had showers and a lounge with a TV. They taught me how to *busk*, as they called it, or beg, as others call it. We would stand on the street, holding a sign with Sharpied pleas, hoping people would show sympathy and give us the change from the bottom of their pockets. Ace realized I would be an asset in this regard. "We'll make a lot more because you're so young and people will feel bad for you," he encouraged. And he was right.

One day I asked Star to take me to the library so I could use the computer. She agreed and we hopped on the next bus downtown. Once there, I sat down at a station a few computers away from Star, who was applying for jobs, and logged into my email, searching to see if my parents had replied to my messages. Nothing. Not a word.

My fingers furiously pounded out an email, enraged at the complete disregard. "*Well, aren't you going to look for me? Do you even care? Why haven't you replied?*" I conveniently overlooked—or willfully disregarded—what I had written in my last email, telling them never to look for me and not to bother contacting me. I was a mental and emotional mess. Trying to keep my cool, I logged off and told Star I was finished. *How could my parents not reply to my last* [hateful] *email?!*

That night, back at Mamma's apartment, I stood at the stove, stirring a pot of ramen. My internal vortex of feelings mirrored the motion of the noodles. Moments later my external situation would be swept into the cyclone as well.

"Angel, come in the living room please. I need to speak with you." Mamma's voice was sticky.

"One second. I'm finishing making my ramen," I called back.

"No, now. Star, finish making her ramen."

Mamma was boss, and I felt obligated to follow her orders. The storm was brewing. My rebellious streak had been stoked. Parental authority, no matter where it came from, was my adversary. *I ran away to be free, NOT to be told what to do anymore.* I could hold my peace for now, but could also sense that a battle was not far off.

"Come here, Angel. Sit down and please don't freak out." she started. "We have found out some things about you and this Bob Von Baron guy. I understand he made you call him God." *What? Wait. . . . What?* I had blended into this pseudo family so quickly that I had almost forgotten about the lie that had gained me access. But now it seemed like she was falling into the delusion with me. *Does she just WANT to lie? To join the lie? I'm confused.* I had no clue where she was going with this, but if she wanted to expand the lie, I would just go with it. It was actually kind of exciting. *Where was this going to go?* Having no clue, I nodded my head yes, that this made-up prostitution ring leader had made me call him God.

"Well, he's put out a bounty on your head for $250,000." *Wait, is she trying to trap me? Is she toying with me? The guy isn't real.* Suddenly a different thought made me pause. The character might not be real, but his name was. When I conjured him into existence, I had borrowed a name from one of the guys I had chatted with online years ago. *Could this be the same guy?* Had Mamma somehow found the real Bob Von Baron? *No! Bob Von Baron isn't a real name either . . . that guy would have been using a fake name online . . . wouldn't he? This is nuts.*

Regardless of what was going on, I fed into her promptings. "What!?" I pretended to panic and started to breathe heavily.

"Don't panic. It's okay. You remember Brandon from the park the other day?"

"Yes, I do. The one with the giant ass."

Mamma laughed and nodded her head. "He's coming to stay with us and help protect you. He'll be with you all the time. Now, I will warn you. He is gay and will flirt with you. Do not, I repeat, do *not* let him touch you. I forbid it." I had no idea what this game was, but I was in it. I remember thinking I had just won the lottery.

That night Brandon came over to Mamma's with a big suitcase and a bigger bag of weed. We all hung out, smoking ourselves into oblivion. I remember going to bed on the futon with Brandon on the floor beside me, thinking, *Don't let him touch me? Ha! It's not him she should be worried about.*

Over the course of the next two days Brandon and I became very close. We went on walks through the park and played video games together. On one of our walks, his arm slid casually around my shoulders. As he started to rub my shoulder, I immediately became aroused. He noticed. "Oh!" he said with a smile, "Someone is excited," as he pushed me playfully in front of him and pulled me in for a hug.

"I'm sorry." I quickly replied as my face turned as burgundy as my hair.

"Oh please, It's normal. Let's be honest here. I've noticed the way you've been looking at me. It's cute." I blushed even more. "Want to do something about it?"

Embarrassment and excitement washed over me, and I blurted out the truth. "Yes."

"Alright then. Let's do something about it."

We made our way to a public park bathroom nearby. This fulfilled fantasy was a passageway to an unfolding future nightmare. Though

I had a bit of so-called experience, I was essentially green. Brandon pulled out a pipe, the shape of which was familiar from my recent escapades with Mike in Chicago.

"You ever try crystal?" Brandon asked with a tempting smirk on his face.

"Love that shit," I replied, knowing exactly what was about to happen: mind-blowing sex and a ticket to impending disaster.

By the time we walked into Mamma's house, all the lights were off, and all was quiet. He called out to see if anyone was home. No one replied. "Want to go again?" Without hesitation I jumped up into his arms and threw my legs around him, kissing him firmly. We lay down on the futon and proceeded, rough and passionate.

Out of nowhere, Mamma screamed from the kitchen, "What the fuck do you think you're doing?!" Brandon threw me off so fast that I fell from the futon and landed on the floor, legs flying over my head. As if transported to Eden, we grasped frantically for blankets to cover ourselves, as Mamma prepared to cast us out. "*Get dressed and get the fuck out, Brandon!*" She continued. "You had *one* job to do. Protect Angel, not fuck him!"

Brandon threw on his clothes as quickly as he had taken them off and raced out the door. Less a snake and more a chameleon actor, I immediately turned on the tears.

"I didn't want to!" I cried. "He was so forceful."

Mamma ran over and again wrapped her arms around me. "I know, baby, I know." My deception had her fooled.

I never saw Brandon again. That door had shut, but another one had opened. He might have opened it and invited me in, but I had walked through willingly. The drugs kept me up all night.

I was still high when morning came. I could hear Mamma crying in her bedroom. She was on the phone. "I understand. Thank you for letting me know." Her sobs were all-consuming, large, almost to the point of unbelievable. She came out of her room and made her way down the hall toward the kitchen. I walked over and stood in the doorway looking at her.

"What's wrong?" I asked gently.

"Sit down, baby," Mamma replied. "Mamma's got some bad news." She pointed to the little round patio dining table she had in the kitchen. I did as I was told and quietly sat down.

"I told some of the guys what had happened to you with Brandon. They took care of it." She wept. Confusion and horror clutched my diaphragm.

"What do you mean, they took care of it?" I asked slowly, hoping for details that might shed light on the seriousness of her claim. *Did she mean they talked to him? Beat him up?*

"They took care of it. You won't be hurt by him again." *Killed him?* "Not only has he hurt others but he squealed on you as a runaway last night. He contacted Bob Van Baron. He told him where you were. This goes against the Juggalos' code. Some of the other guys in our family have been wanting to do this to Brandon for a while, but never had enough reason. He won't be coming back to hurt you any-more." Lies begetting lies. Without saying anything else she stood up, brushed away her fake tears, handed me a bowl to smoke, and went back into her bedroom.

For a moment my head swirled with mental calculations. *Had they found the guy I had chatted with online? No, it couldn't be. There is no way that Bob Von Baron was his real name; he was just some random guy I chatted with online. There is no prostitution ring. This is a JOKE! She likes her own lies!*

My disbelief was growing. I began to realize that Mamma needed her own stories to feel power. This was her control. Either all of them believe my lie of a story, or they believe Mamma's lies and are sharing a delusion, or they don't and are addicted to the drama themselves and are just going along with it for their own entertainment. But *Brandon. . . . Did she mean what I thought she meant? Did they expel him or worse? Did they kill him?* The hair stood up on every inch of my body. I knew that I couldn't be a part of this charade any longer. I knew . . . *I have to run!*

Almost 20 minutes later Mamma came out of her room and looked as if nothing ever happened. "Alright, I'm on my way to work. I'm leaving you my cell phone. You don't leave this house. Lock the doors and don't let anyone inside who doesn't already have a key. Here's my phone number at work. You call me if anything happens that makes you feel unsafe." She handed me a piece of paper with her work number on it, then gave me a hug and walked out the door, locking it behind her.

My plan formed quickly. *I have to go to Las Vegas. It's the closest and biggest city near here.* I packed my belongings with lightning speed, then slowed with the realization that I needed bus fare. I rushed into Mamma's room and started ransacking it, looking for money. I found a jar under her bed filled with quarters. *Perfect! This will do. I'll exchange the quarters for cash and buy a bus ticket.*

Playing into their embrace of the delusion, I then ransacked the rest of the apartment to make it look like Bob had found me and that there was a struggle. I wrote out a note with a Sharpie on the living room wall: "*You didn't do a very good job protecting him leaving him alone. We have been watching you now for days. He is mine.*" And to add a bit of Mamma's own dramatic embellishment to the lies, I signed it with the fictious perpetrator's fictious alias "*—God.*"

For my final act, to make it look even more real, I took the hatchet that was hanging on the wall in the hallway and struck it into the wall next to the note. Why I did this, I have no idea. Possibly because I was still high and just not in my right mind.

I grabbed my bag and the jar of quarters and darted out the door. I took the back streets toward the downtown bus station. On the way, I stopped at a bank, where I exchanged the quarters for cash. After securing a ticket to Las Vegas, I sat down and waited for three hours for the bus. Doubt resurfaced. Everything was so confusing. I was lost in the ever-deepening untruths. I remembered what Mamma had said to me only hours before. *He won't be hurting you again.* This truly terrified me, though a part of me did not believe it. The relief I had in finding a posse was gone. I realized I didn't truly know any of them, nor what they might be capable of; I only knew that I had to leave. I would find what I was looking for this time, in Las Vegas. I just knew it.

Breathe. Taking advantage of someone not only hurts them but weakens my potential.

Breathe. There is only one outcome for lying: getting caught. I can lie myself silly, but one day the truth will come out and when it does, I will realize lying is never worth it.

Breathe. I can run and run and run, but I will never be able to hide from myself.

14

Las Vegas, Do or Die

Breathe. Sometimes it's better to quit before self-destruction is inevitable.

Breathe. When you find moments of peace and sanity, hold onto them with all your might, for those moments are truly rare and often taken for granted.

Breathe. When the moment of surrender occurs, seize the opportunity. Freedom is on the other side.

The bus to Las Vegas was loaded. I was still disguised as Angel. I sat in my seat, exhausted, makeup smeared and stomach growling. Wearing a skirt, a tube top, and a long burgundy wig I had gotten while staying with the Juggalos, I got up from my seat with my bag and made my way back to the bathroom. I locked the door behind me and began to shuffle through my bag looking for something more comfortable to put on. It was cold on the bus from the blasting AC. I had no warm clothes, so I pulled a out pair of shorts. They were my favorites, a pair of blue shorts that hung just above my knees. I had worn these all the time before I became Angel.

I changed back into my boy clothes and opened up the bathroom window. Through the crack, like a serpent shedding its skin, I threw out my skirt, tube top, and wig as we barreled down the highway at 70 miles per hour. I can only imagine what the people in the cars behind us were thinking as they saw my discarded wig flying past them.

After staring at myself in the mirror, I fixed my makeup and smudged eyeliner as best as I could, then I unlocked the door and made my way down the aisle. I sat back down in the same seat but in a completely different look. The man next to me looked over and whispered, "Someone else is sitting here."

Looking back at him I replied, "I know. It's me." His sudden look of confusion was followed by a slow burn of realization, then a stare of apprehension. He looked away and didn't speak to me again the entire ride.

The bus pulled into the station in Las Vegas. I stepped outside into the dry night air. Its warmth was a relief from the assault of the AC. I immediately began asking strangers, "Which way to the Strip?" and was pointed in the right direction but also warned that it was too far to walk, that I better take a cab. I had only a few dollars at best. Not being able to afford even public transportation, I started to walk. The guideposts for my journey were clear. *All I have to do is head toward the tall buildings in the distance.*

I walked through what seemed to be a pretty sketchy part of town, cutting through people's yards and making a good pace toward the Strip. When I seemed to be halfway, I found myself on a deserted, dimly lit street. Only a few cars passed by. *Maybe they could give me a ride.* I put my hand out, giving the international symbol for hitchhiking.

The first several cars passed without stopping. Then I noticed that one particular car, a black Cadillac, had passed me more than once. On its third time, it slowed down and pulled over. The driver, a middle-aged man, rolled down a tinted window. He looked a bit rough, and spoke with a thick Middle Eastern accent. "Where you going, cutie?" he inquired.

"On my way to the Strip," I replied.

"Hop in. I can take you there."

I circled around the front of the car and got in the passenger seat.

"You're walking through a dangerous part of town," he stated. "What are you up to?"

"I'm just looking to go to the Strip," I quickly replied, hoping he wouldn't ask any more questions. I was starting to sense a weird vibe about him. I put my hand on the door's arm rest and my heart sank. The door handle was missing. I had no way out of this car.

"While you're with me, you want to mess around?" he asked with a leering smile that is etched in my memory. "I can pay you."

This changed the equation. *Did I just get lucky, or am I in danger?* I thought, still looking for the door handle. In the momentary pause before I could respond, he reached over and grabbed my crotch. The recoil of his hand was instant. "What the fuck? Are you a boy or a girl?" His voice changed, becoming more aggressive.

It dawned on me that I was in real danger. I hadn't intended to, but my makeup and burgundy hair had tricked him. "I'm a boy," I replied sheepishly.

"Oh no, man! What the fuck?" he barked. "Get the fuck out of my car!"

He got out of the driver's seat, walked around the front of the car and roughly yanked open the passenger-side door. I quickly got out.

"I'm sorry, I thought you knew and wanted me." I pleaded innocently. He grabbed my shirt and pulled me close to his face.

"Fuck no, I wanted pussy," he hissed. He shoved me backward and I fell to the ground. He walked back around the front of his car, mumbling to himself along the way, "Ugly faggot." He drove off into the night, leaving me a startled and frightened heap on the asphalt.

I sat there on the ground for several minutes, terrified by what had just happened. *He could have killed me. He could have beat me up. I had no way out of his vehicle. No one would have known. He could have taken me anywhere. I am so lucky he let me go.* After picking myself up, I doubled my speed, determined to make it out of this corridor of a street to the towering heights and glowing neon lights of the Strip. After another hour and a half, at around 1 a.m., I entered its swirling eddy of energy, an intoxicating and seductive morass with shadows behind every luminous corner.

I walked up and down the strip about five times, before taking a seat on a bench in front of Caesar's Palace. I sat there for the remainder of the night, watching cars come and go. I was still riding high from the intensity of the previous few days, but my energy slowed. The incandescent colors dulled, the tint of sound blurred, its sharp edges muffled, and the motion of endless passing forms became lugubrious. It was as if some higher power had pulled everything into slow motion. I watched as the marquees' LED lights flickered green and black before changing colors, my vision going in and out of focus in rhythm with my awareness, intermittently revealing images of half-naked women advertising sex. Here, flesh printed on postcards; there, flesh on billboards. I saw myself in those exposed women. I had been trying to get started in their trade, but the reality of what that might be was pummeling my mind much like my nightmares had. I was weary with the effects of exhaustion and withdrawal. What was now rammed into my psyche was that I would not just be opening myself to likely physical hammerings and mental thrashings, but also the sale of my soul.

Feeling out of my mind, I started screaming repeatedly at the provocative images on the mobile billboards of the trucks passing by. "*What does your mother think of you?*" Over and over, I cursed the sex workers in these overt displays, shaming myself through their images.

As the night moved on and I roamed the Strip, the flip-flops on my feet began to cut into the skin between my toes. I took them off and continued walking barefoot. Sweat flowed from my pores, releasing pungent toxins.

The sun began to rise as I continued walking up and down the strip aimlessly. Vegas is a town of the night. At this early hour though, the streets were basically deserted. I stumbled upon the Trevi Fountain replica at Caesar's Palace and sat down on its walls, but respite was not reprieve. Being stationary on a windless morning allowed a stagnant olfactory prison to form; my own smell was inescapable. I looked around to see if anyone was coming.

I tucked myself in the corner of the fountain, against a wall. Then one foot after the other I stepped into the fountain. As quickly as I could, I scrubbed my feet and armpits. As the dirt released from my feet, it started to turn the water gray. I surveyed the nearby area again, and quickly surmised that the coast was clear. Like the people I saw bathing outside the Salt Lake City library, I dropped my shorts and underwear and tossed them on the fountain wall. I quickly plunged my bottom into the cold water, scrubbing my crotch and behind. The stealthy bath was complete. As quickly as I got into the fountain, I got out and got dressed again. I couldn't believe that I had gotten away with it. I looked around again and noticed a security camera pointed in my general direction. I pulled my flip-flops out of my bag and put them on again, then flipped off the camera and headed down the street.

By afternoon, my flip-flops had broken and I was back to bare feet. The dirt quickly reaccumulated from walking on the filthy sidewalks, littered with filthy postcards advertising filthy sex. Sex was everywhere, but not one gay club in sight. *How am I going to find someone to take me in and take care of me?* This idea seemed more and more impossible. As my quest for a protector faded, I faced a choice: I could turn myself in or I could kill myself.

The thought of killing myself hit me in a way it hadn't in the past. I was serious this time, still insistent I would never return home. I looked at the dizzying heights of the buildings that encircled me. The carnival of garish colors and enticing designs laughed like a deranged cotton-candy pusher, pleading for attention but delivering only sweet sickness. *How do I get up there so I can jump? Or do I just walk in front of a truck?*

I entered the lobby of the Mandalay Bay hotel and scanned the lobby walls for stairway access. No luck. I began to walk along the building corridors searching for the stairs. Maybe they were there, but I couldn't find them. Feeling completely defeated, I gave up and walked back outside.

Out of nowhere, I began sobbing. The pain I was causing myself, the excruciating mental anguish, the agony of coming down from drugs, the torment of pure exhaustion. I paused.

I looked up to the sky and inhaled, taking a deep breath. *Do or die.* For some reason my mind switched. Everything became clear, as if I were back in my right mind. *You can't kill yourself; there is so much more life to live. You are just going down the wrong road. You need a U-turn. Turn yourself in.*

I ran across Las Vegas Boulevard and up the street to a gas station. Feeling myself close to the edge of passing out, I grabbed a Mountain Dew from the coolers along the wall. I opened the can and began to chug, without hesitating. The store clerk noticed what I was doing and shouted, "Hey you have to pay for that!" I looked back at him as I made my way out the door and shouted, "You will make the money back, trust me," and I dashed out the door feeling no shame or guilt about this.

How do I turn myself in? Where can I be safe? Go to the airport, I thought to myself. *Airports are safe.* I would have to walk. Once I finally made it inside the main terminal, I looked around for a pay phone. I had only 55 cents to my name, not enough to call long distance. A woman was sitting nearby, using her cell phone. I walked over and sat a few seats away, waiting for her to finish her phone call. As she hung up, I stood up and walked over to her.

"Hi, umm, can I use your cell phone to call home?" I asked her, both of us aware of my sorry state. She looked me up and down, noticing the dirt on my legs and my blackened bare feet.

"No, I'm sorry. I can't help you." I wouldn't have been surprised if she assumed this was a ploy to steal her phone, but I needed to make that call, so I refused to go away.

"I beg you. Please, I have fifty-five cents. I need to call my parents and let them know where I am at and that I am okay." I continued to plead. I could see her making an assessment of the risk, looking me up and down again. It was clear she was circumspect. Finally, after what felt like forever, she made her decision, chose kindness (or pity), and handed me her phone.

"Make it quick, I have a flight to catch," she remarked, setting a protective boundary in case she changed her mind.

"Oh, thank you, thank you!" I said to her as I punched in the phone number for home. Ring. . . .Ring. . .Ring. . .

"Hello?" My sister Sonia answered the phone.

"Is Mom there?" I quickly asked. There was a moment of pause.

"Bruce?" She asked. "Is that you?"

"Yes, it's me. Is Mom there?" I started to snap.

"Yes, just a moment. . . . . Mom, it's Bruce," she called out. Again, a moment of pause, then a familiar voice.

"Bruce?" Mom asked hopefully.

"Yeah, it's me." I began to cry a cry of relief.

"It is so good to hear your voice," she replied. "Where are you?"

"In Las Vegas. I'm at the airport. I want to come home." I answered.

"You have to turn yourself in. Find a police officer and turn yourself in."

The instruction felt like relief. "I will. I promise."

"Do it, Bruce. You have to." She reassured me that I was going to be okay but that I had to do this, no delay.

I hung up and returned the phone to the woman, who was clearly confused. I cried again, thanking her repeatedly through my fast-flowing tears, then I headed for an information booth.

"Hi, I need to speak with a police officer," I quickly exclaimed. A type of unidentifiable eagerness was forming.

"Why?" the clerk said with a bit of an attitude.

"Because I am a 16-year-old runaway prostitute and I need to go home," I shot back at her.

"Oh! Okay."

A few minutes later an officer came my way and took me aside. I explained my situation to him; however, I was still not in my right mind, so I gave him my sob story, the lie, in full detail, complete with running away from a prostitution ring. I thought this would spare me some of the consequences I suspected were in store.

He took me to a holding room in the airport where we were met by a few more officers, including an FBI agent and an officer working for Las Vegas Vice. I shared my sob story again, this time to him. After listening carefully to my bull cocky, they sent me to a youth shelter until my father could, once again, fly down and pick me up. The vice officer called my parents and relayed my story. He even tried to convince my parents that I was telling the truth.

Two days passed before my father flew down and picked me up from the shelter. He was even quieter than the last time. As we got off the plane in Butte and made our way to the tiny airport lobby, I don't know what I was really expecting. I had stolen my parents' car and money, and run away for the second time. Clearly, I was in trouble.

There were two police officers waiting. My dad grabbed my bag, and the officers grabbed me. I was placed in handcuffs and shackles as my dad stepped back and sadly watched me struggle to walk to the back of the squad car. Then he went home.

It was a 35-minute drive before we arrived at the juvenile detention center, RYO, in Galen, Montana. This is where I would spend the next 59 days. I was furious with myself and rightfully so. While I was there, my mom and dad visited, and so did Mellie from Same Difference theater company. I would be on one side of the glass with them on the other, and we would speak through a phone on a very short metal cord. When my mom came to visit, I was filled with rage that was directed entirely at her. Looking at her through the glass, I would think about Berna and then I'd fill with the fear that I was never really wanted. My distorted relationship with authority compounded my anger toward her. She had been on plenty of prison visits, having gone through it with her own family and even some of my siblings. This was something she had never wanted to repeat. It was just too painful for her. And yet, here we were. I had disappointed her. When she told me that she hated to come to RYO and wouldn't visit again, I was full of shame and guilt, and the sense of being abandoned again.

I continued to lie to everyone about why I was locked up. I still couldn't face the truth, so I kept giving my now-familiar sob story of the prostitution ring I was running away from. My parents, of course, didn't buy it at all.

On the 59th day, I had a court hearing in Butte. My parents watched me struggle to walk into the courtroom in handcuffs and shackles. The judge heard my case and detailed the charges against me. It was agreed that with willing and good behavior, I would be released into a group home for troubled youth. This is where I would live for the next seven months.

I don't think it is too much to say, that by a series of miracles, I had survived the summer. Despite all the drugs, the dark and scary alley-ways, and the abuse I inflicted on myself and suffered from others, I lived. I survived. I made it back to where I started. I had been heading down the wrong path. I made my U-turn and, without fail, it brought me back to exactly where I needed to be.

The staff at the home for troubled youth didn't put up with much of anything. If you cursed, you faced consequences; if you fought, you faced even worse consequences. However, I was particularly well behaved and earned privileges fairly quickly. I earned the ability to have occasional weekends at home, to go for walks outside by myself, to participate in extracurricular activities, and even to have a radio and DVD player in my room.

It was still summer when I entered the group home, but the school year was fast approaching. Regular high school was no longer an option. I was informed that, because of my criminal record, I would need to complete my junior year, and possibly my senior year, at the alternative high school. I had no choice, so I followed along willingly.

During my stay at the group home, I was also enrolled in the dance academy, directly across the street. My parents thought I would benefit from it in a variety of ways. Most importantly, it demanded much more discipline than what they could give me. I took to it with relish and quickly discovered that I had a natural talent for it. I studied ballet, tap, lyrical, contemporary, jazz, and some musical theatre, and thrived in them all. I spent the first half of each day in school, and directly after, spent the rest of each day in many dance classes.

While the dance was great, there were still consequences for my actions. I was placed on probation, and ordered to serve 200 hours of community service, which I was sure would be miserable. Fortunately, there was no garbage pickup. Instead, I was assigned to work in the local soup kitchen, where I helped prepare food or was put to work waxing the floors. The locals who came to the kitchen for their daily lunch or dinner were very sweet and generous people. All it took was a moment to get to know them a little better. The experience really changed my view of homeless people. Before, I would just put them all in a mental box, labeling them as drug users or drunks. I imagined that they chose to be homeless, and given my youth, the irony of my judgment had been lost. It took virtually no time to learn that my assumptions were wrong. I was amazed and embarrassed at how wrong I had been. I also learned that my assumptions were those of a snob, and that I had forgotten my own misadventures so quickly. I had forgotten where I had just been, and also where I had started as an infant, going from rags to riches. Never had I thought that people could become homeless simply because they couldn't keep up or afford their living situations. Some had simply lost their job and fallen behind; others had had sicknesses that were beyond their control.

This experience provided me with a great deal of additional discipline, as well as a dose of humility, and a new level of gratitude for my life and the privileges I had been afforded. It was here, in a punishment enacted for the indulgences of selfishness and impetuous self-destructive behavior, that an idea formed for something that was its polar opposite. Helping others seemed to serve me well in my recovery journey and sparked the dream of becoming a motivational speaker, although this goal wouldn't be achieved for many years. After seeing speakers come to our school assemblies to share their own stories of hope, recovery, and inspiration, I sensed that someday I could do the same. I had many battles yet to fight, but I had seen the old familiar path my father described, and perhaps I would find my way onto it.

Breathe. Sometimes it's better to quit before my self-destruction is inevitable.

Breathe. When I find moments of peace and sanity, I will hold onto them with all my might, for those moments are truly rare and often taken for granted.

Breathe. When the moment of surrender occurs, I will seize the opportunity. Freedom is on the other side.

15

On My Way

Breathe. You'll be amazed by what you can accomplish when you rigorously show up for yourself.

Breathe. People may not be what they appear to be at first impressions, but when they show their true colors the first time, believe them.

Breathe. People, places, and things have a huge effect on your judgment and actions in life. Be very careful where you put your energy and who you surround yourself with.

Breathe, and keep moving forward.

By the grace of the higher powers that be, I graduated from high school. Given the chaos of my life to that point, I considered my final GPA of 3.6 pretty darn good for a person who also had learning disabilities and a desire to hate school. I joked that I graduated as valedictorian because I had the highest GPA of my small class of six other students at the alternative high school. But I did, in fact, take pride in this point. I was headed in the right direction.

Other areas of my life were taking shape as well. I had taken a job and was saving my money as much as possible, preparing to make a big move to New York. This dream had been launched years ago when I was acting in *Oliver*, and it was finally within reach. I had managed to save $6,700, which didn't seem like much considering that New York is one of the most expensive cities in the world, but it was enough for me to pull it off. Much of the mental and chemical madness that came from drug use and the hormones from puberty had stabilized. My obsession for sex had subsided. I was on a medication that helped with my bipolar disorder, and the discipline of dance and study was keeping me more focused on my real-life goals.

October 1, 2009, was the chosen date for my departure, and I could hardly wait. I remember showing up at the airport where an assembly of my friends and most of my family were waiting to see me off. The tears we cried as we embraced were of genuine joy, anticipation, and pride rather than the silent tears of sadness, dread, anxious confused desperation, and shame of previous airport reunions. We didn't know when we would be seeing each other again, but this time there was hope and a level of shared confidence.

After our final farewells, I made my way through security and got on the plane. A fingernail's worth of an old familiar feeling carved its way in. The doubt was only temporary, but these thoughts had been here before, just like in my nightmares on the bus. In those brief moments, alone again, I strengthened my resolve. This time I was not running away from something, but rather running toward a goal. I had worked hard for this. My life was full of possibility. I would not be defined by my past.

When I landed at JFK International Airport, I cried in happiness. A lifetime dream was coming true. I headed to the baggage claim, but my newfound delight was short lived. The people who had been on my flight slowly started to disappear with their bags, but my luggage had not arrived. I felt lost in a mechanical sound bath of pulsing lights and moving metal. I was alone in an unknown place, whose rules and rhythms I didn't understand. Nothing I packed up for my new life in the big city had made it, not my clothes nor my *Will and Grace* DVDs. After checking at the lost baggage office with no success, I was instructed to follow up daily. Two weeks later, I was finally reunited with my belongings, but for now I would have to get by with my wits, and whatever was in my backpack and carry on.

I took a cab to the apartment I had arranged in Harlem. I started up the street from the corner of 150th Street and Frederick Douglass Boulevard. *You got this, Bruce.* Unexpectedly, a man shouted directly at me, "Someone's gonna get his ass beat!" I have been verbally accosted many times because my flamboyance and ebullient energy is in no way understated. I ran up the street toward the apartment and knocked franticly on the door. My friend Landen, also from Montana, opened it. We had performed in numerous stage shows together and had been seeking to manifest this move for several years. While I had flown, he had taken the long train ride about a week earlier.

"I'm gonna get my ass beat!" I shouted as I flew past him and slammed the door behind me.

"Wow, okay, welcome to New York." Landen said in a friendly but confused manner.

Three days later, I got my first job in the city, at a Starbucks in Times Square. Its ceaseless frenetic pace was a far cry from the candy shop in Virginia City, and I absolutely hated the job. It was a 24-hour express Starbucks with a line out the door at all hours. The New Yorkers and tourists it served were always in a rush, expecting their coffee to be made before they even walked in.

Landen and I spent the first two weeks touring the city with the woman we were subletting from. We had found her listing through an ad online. Upon meeting her in person, we clicked instantly. She was a jazz singer from London who was gearing up for a move to Las Vegas for a show and would be leaving the apartment shortly. The plan was that we would be overlapping with her in the space for only a short time before she left. The apartment was a miniscule one-bedroom with a bathroom the size of a dining table. Landen and I shared a full-sized bed in the bedroom, while she and her pit bull, Max, slept in the living room on a pullout couch. It was crowded but, at first, being with her was a pleasure. She arranged a private walking tour of Harlem for us, and she took me to some of the jazz clubs where she performed.

Even though she had promised that she would be moving out, she said there was a slight delay, but we quickly realized that we were being scammed. She had no intention of moving out. She didn't. She was in fact freeloading with us paying the rent and her just staying put. The boxes stacked in the living room were empty. When we confronted her, she promptly became cold to us and started adding random fees for everything, even using the outlets to charge our phones.

The following two weeks were hell; her attitude and behavior were night and day from the woman we initially met. We walked on eggshells around her, until one day I got a call at work from Landen. "We are leaving this dump. I found us a hostel we can stay at not too far from here," he said.

Managing a comical amalgamation of tightly packed suitcases and a huge, overstuffed duffel bag, we piled into a subway car and made our way to the hostel, where we would be staying for the next two weeks, or so I thought.

I got another phone call from Landen while I was at work the next day. "I'm sorry, but I don't think being here in New York is for me. I'm on the next flight out," he admitted nervously.

I tried to sound confident and supportive in my reply, but fear and frustration surged inside me. *I am going to be all alone in this city that I truly know nothing about.* We said our goodbyes and early the next morning he was gone. I spent the next two weeks looking for another place to live. After searching all over Craigslist for options that would fit my meager budget, I found an ad for a room for rent downtown next to the South Street Seaport in the Financial District. With my dwindling funds, the price was right; however, even I knew it was simply too good to be true. I called the phone number listed in the ad to investigate. An older gentleman named Charles picked up the phone. We spoke for several minutes and agreed to meet that evening.

Charles was a very skinny, elderly gay man who wore his gray hair parted firmly to one side. He had big eyes that were wide open, and he greeted me warmly. He seemed like a nice guy. We walked inside and made our way up to the ninth floor. He showed me around his space. It was a nice two-bedroom apartment with an amazing view overlooking the Seaport and the Brooklyn Bridge. He showed me the bedroom for rent, which had two twin beds in it. On one of the beds was a handsome young man, funnily enough, named Landon. We talked for several minutes before more of the details were revealed. It wasn't the bedroom I would be renting. He was renting the couch in the living room for $400 a month. *It's better than nothing, I guess.* There were three rules to living there:

No women are allowed.
You mustn't answer the door if anyone knocks.
You must have a good time and go out for drinks with him on occasion.

I could do that, no problem.

I optimistically packed my things and moved into my life downtown. Living in a house full of gay men in the middle of the Financial District was sort of a dream come true for me. Over the first few months, I got to know Manhattan well and kept focused on my goals. I moved to New York City to become a performer. In that pursuit, I took dance classes frequently at Broadway Dance Center and was auditioning often. There was a certain poetry to it. I was living the novel life of a struggling artist. The reality was a bit more difficult. With what I was making from Starbucks, I barely had enough to keep up with rent, food, transportation, and my dance classes. Paying for anything else was just not an option.

I plugged on for six months, working at the coffee shop and hating it more with each passing day. I eventually quit. Charles told me he could get me a job dancing as a go-go boy at Stonewall, where we went together regularly. We met his friend, the bartender, and that same night I auditioned as a dancer. *I loved it.* Something sparked inside of me that I hadn't felt since I had run away from home. Years had passed, but it was back. I relished the sexual passion and power that I felt while showing my perfect dance moves to the crowd. Sexy gyrations caused the men to drool and put money in my shorts. It was an amazing night. But I found out that I did not get the job because I was too skinny for the role they were looking for. While I might not have been the muscle hunk that Stonewall wanted, I found work at other bars, go-going for Twink Tuesdays at a well-known Chelsea watering hole and also at a hotspot in up-and-coming Long Island City.

Despite having work, I had no idea how to budget my money. Life in New York was a constant financial struggle. I started to take any odd job that I could find, still trying to make it work.

I got word that Kathleen, who had stood up for me all those years ago in Twin Bridges, was moving to New York very soon. When she arrived several weeks later, we met up for dinner at the Subway just around the corner. It was fun and familiar, and made the city feel a little less overwhelming. In the months that followed, we would meet up to enjoy walking adventures together. I was constantly broke and always stressed, but it was a wonderful time to be in the city.

During this time I met a guy named Paul. We had connected via Craigslist Personals. Our first real-world interaction took place in Central Park, and I quickly fell madly in love with him. When he introduced me to some of his friends, I knew I had found my new posse. We hung out all the time, and I wanted to fit in. Since they all smoked weed, I quickly lost my willpower and started to smoke weed too. I gravitated to one of them who was also a professional dancer. Spencer was a tall young man with dark brown hair who was also adopted. We hit it off right away and quickly became inseparable. Spencer and I faced the same challenges. Like me, he couldn't keep a job and truly couldn't afford anything, so it wasn't long before he needed a place to live. Inviting him to live at Charles's was practically a foregone conclusion, so I brought him home to share the pullout sofa bed, and also the small amount of monthly rent. We would share this bed for the months to come.

Having quit Starbucks, I was working at a chocolate shop in the West Village, and like always, I began to hate it. One night, as I was closing up shop and counting the cash from the register, I slipped a $5 bill in my pocket to help me get home. I was fired the next day. I didn't yet recognize that I was starting to stray from my familiar path because attention was focused on the more immediate needs. Once again, I was on the hunt for employment. Luckily, I found a job fairly quickly at a tanning salon. They hired me as an airbrush artist, to give spray tans to clients all day. Since I had quite the history of art on my resume, it seemed like a good fit, and it was.

Spencer and I started tagging along with several other guys who worked at the tanning salon, going out with them after work and on the weekends. It only took a little contraband to get me into the clubs that I wasn't associated with. Spencer gave me a fake ID and we were good for entry. At one of these clubs, Splash, a coworker offered me a bump of cocaine. Without even thinking, I took it, put it up to my nose, and snorted it in. Then another, followed by another. That night, the music thumped loudly and the green laser lights beamed across the dance floor, creating stripes in the darkness. The fog morphed and broke their expanse, creating a seductive shadow show. The lights merged and separated from a single beam to a pantheon array in time to the music, hypnotizing me and the undulating mass of fellow dancers. I would return to this queer cathedral seeking its promises of ecstasy many times. My old habits were back, and I was heading down the wrong road. This cycle of partying continued for months.

One night, after having way too many drinks and way too much cocaine, my stomach began to twist. I needed to run to the bathroom *now* or I was going to shit myself. I stumbled through the crowd, fighting my way to the bathroom, which was long and dark and lit by blacklight, creating a disorienting glow. One wall was lined with urinal stalls and the other with toilet stalls. Some of the urinals were separated by black partitions and others by see-through glass, allowing for discreet exhibitionism. I staggered hastily into a stall, closed the door, and locked it, about to explode. After my bout of intestinal distress was resolved, I looked up to find that there was no toilet paper. It's not that it had run out, but that there wasn't even a place to put it. As I looked to my left, a face stared back at me, mouth agape in disgust, his eyes wide with horror. It was then that I realized my mistake. I had just taken a shocking shit in a urinal with a strange man watching me. I instantly sobered up and wanted to die. I pulled up my pants without zipping or buttoning them, walked wide-legged across the hall to the toilet side and shut the door, shuddering in shame. I tried my best to clean myself, then waited several minutes, hoping that the unlucky stranger had left the bathroom. I walked out with my head down, washed my hands and then bolted back to the dance floor looking frantically for Spencer. When I found him at last, I grabbed him by the arm and shouted, "We have to leave! Now!"

We left the club and started walking up the street, with the music fading in the distance. Worried, Spencer waited till we were a few steps down the street and then asked, "Bruce, what the hell just happened? I was having fun."

"Not me," I snapped back and then I relayed what had just happened. Without hesitating, Spencer doubled over, laughing uncontrollably.

"It's not funny!" I said, trying not to laugh myself, and trying to cultivate insistence. "I can never go back there."

We went back the next night.

Nights like this became more and more frequent. My willpower to resist drugs had faded, and my drive had as well. By the time I even noticed, it had been six months since I had auditioned for anything or taken dance lessons. In that awareness, I had a chance to find my way back to the familiar path, but instead I decided, *Screw it. I'll just have fun.*

After two years living with Charles, I was able to save up enough money to get my own apartment in Brooklyn, just on the edge of Park Slope. Paul and I had been dating for almost a year at this point, and my new place was just a few blocks from his apartment. Paul and I loved each other, but I think we loved the sex more. We had a wild, out-of-this-world type of chemistry. We were mainly addicted to each other, but sometimes we would have strangers join us. Unfortunately, Paul and I wouldn't last. We were cheating on each other constantly, which meant we were always lying to each other. And eventually, we were always fighting.

Paul and my problems didn't stop me from having fun though. Spencer and I kept indulging as free spirits, going out and going heavy as two young gay men in their 20s living in New York City. We frequently went online to look for guys to have three-ways with.

One night we met a guy named Felik who lived in Chelsea. He was a well-known stylist with plenty of money to insulate him from many of the dangers of his excesses. Rather than leading to a hallway of apartment doors, the elevator went straight to his apartment foyer. Felik was waiting to greet us. The apartment was a chic space with modern furniture and pricey sculptures. As we walked through his long apartment, he led us back to his bedroom where two other guys were already engaged in a naked escapade. We talked briefly, then quickly got down to business. Eventually, the two other men left, and Spencer passed out on the bed. Felik invited me to another bedroom, at the front of the apartment, and brought a little black leather bag with him.

I lay on the bed, relaxing after the previous moments filled with passionate anonymous sex. Felik opened the leather bag and pulled out a glass pipe. My heart exploded. I could feel my pupils blacken like a shark's when they smell blood. I knew exactly what that was.

"Have you ever tried crystal?" Felik asked as he poured some of the rocks into the pipe, loading it up.

"Yes, I have but it's been a few years," I replied. I couldn't stop myself. "Can I have some?"

I awoke the beast.

Breathe. I will be amazed by what I can accomplish when I rigorously show up for myself.

Breathe. People may not be what they appear to be at first impressions, but when they show me their true colors the first time, I will believe them.

Breathe. People, places, and things have a huge effect on my judgment and actions in life. I will be very careful where I put my energy and who I surround myself with.

Breathe, and keep moving forward.

16

The Diagnoses

Breathe. When your body is telling you that something is wrong, listen to it. Your body won't lie to you.

Breathe. The darkest times in your life have so many windows of hope and opportunity. Try not to be discouraged, for there are answers.

Breathe. Sometimes it might feel like you are at the end with no hope in sight. But it is amazing how the will to survive kicks in when you run out of options.

Breathe, and keep moving forward.

Felik embodied what I had been looking for years ago when I ran away: a loving, rich, sexy older man who would use me as he pleased, but also take care of me. I was practically living with him. Used, abused, and loved, I relived my early trauma. It seemed perfect; I was having the illusionary time of my life. Instead of the glow of new love, my relationship kept my eyes dilated and raccooned with dark circles.

I staggered through my shifts spray-tanning my clients, and managing not to pass out thanks to an ever-available bump of cocaine from one of my coworkers. I can only imagine what some of these clients must have thought of me, darting all over the salon and twitching uncontrollably.

Toward the end of my second year working at the tanning salon, I started to become sick. Each day I noticed an incremental increase in my discomfort. Under normal circumstances, when I felt unwell I would just get sick for a day or two and then I would get better. However, this felt different, and it wasn't going away. Two bumps started to form in my armpits. I didn't know what that meant. After three weeks of feeling every muscle aching in pain, I finally took myself to a clinic to get some help. The entire way there I subconsciously thought to myself, *You are dying, you are dying.*

"What brings you in today?" the nurse asked. I told her my symptoms and that I felt like death warmed over.

"You look like death warmed over," she agreed. I was hunched over. If I tried to stand completely straight, I would double over in distress. I was constantly sweating and the feeling of fever was ever-present. Every joint and muscle in my body screamed in agony. My veins felt as though I had nothing in them. I could feel my heartbeat in my toes and my breathing had become very shallow. The nurse took samples of my blood to run various tests.

The wait for results intensified my pain. I just wanted to be home in Park Slope and on my air mattress under huge thick blankets. About 30 minutes went by, then my number was called again. I went back into the examination room. This time there was an additional nurse and a doctor. I knew something was seriously wrong.

"Hi, Bruce. Why don't you sit down here for me?" With a little help from the nurse, I managed to take a seat.

There was not even a moment of hesitation from the doctor. I was still adjusting myself on the examination table when he blurted out coldly, "Your rapid test results came back positive for HIV." His words were quick and devoid of emotion. "Your viral load is dangerously high and your CD4 count is basically nonexistent. Here are some brochures for you to look over and here are some referrals to clinics that you should follow up with."

Your rapid test results came back positive for HIV. He had announced it like he was telling me that I had ketchup on my shirt.

I went into shock. It was so devastating, I couldn't even cry. I had no energy to do so. "What is a viral load and CD4 count?" I asked.

"The viral load is the amount of the virus that is in a person's bloodstream and the CD4 count (T cells) means the number of white blood cells that help fight off infection in the bloodstream. In your case, your viral load is so high that you are borderline having progressed to AIDS, the disease that HIV can turn into if it goes untreated."

I left the clinic with my information packets and my diagnosis. Upon stepping outside the clinic doors, it was as if I lost my hearing. The world went quiet. The continuous hum of the city was gone. No blaring horns, no conversations from passersby, no screeching brakes, no rumbling trucks, not one squawking bird was to be heard. Silence, pure silence, seemed to fill my ears.

The first thing I did was to go to the corner store and buy a pack of cigarettes. I stood in front of it smoking five cigarettes in a row. This didn't make me feel any better. I made it back to my apartment in Brooklyn by taking the train, an indefinite eternity. Once back in my room, I collapsed on my air mattress, which had slowly deflated. The floodgates opened and I just started sobbing. I grabbed my phone and called my parents back home in Montana and told them the news the second they answered. It was a very short phone call because I couldn't stop crying. My parents endeavored to reassure me that everything was going to be okay and that they would be coming out to see me. I hung up the phone, unrelieved, and cried until I fell asleep.

Over the next few days, a dreaded obligation unfolded. I had to call my most recent sexual partners to let them know, so that they too could get tested. For the one-night stands I had phone numbers for, this was pretty easy. Telling Paul was harder, and telling Felik was very difficult. We were still spending time together, but I realized I didn't know him that well and I couldn't imagine what his reaction would be.

When I did break the news, he reassured me that everything was going to be fine. He had seen the worst of the AIDS epidemic as well as the advancements in treatment throughout the years. That is one of the surprising things that I encountered repeatedly as I made those calls. Instead of being angry at me or afraid of me, most people wanted to be there for me and showed it by listening and being very understanding.

Within three weeks, my parents were on their way to visit and attempt to cheer me up. During the time before their arrival, I had gotten set up at a clinic with a primary care doctor who helped me to navigate getting full coverage health insurance and government assistance. In New York State, the benefits for people living with HIV are completely humane, a model of compassion and understanding. I was able to get food stamps, weekly financial assistance, and housing assistance.

I was soon placed on my first cocktail of medications to combat the HIV virus. It wasn't immediate, but after some time I started to feel a bit better, though I still had a long way to go. When my parents came, as promised, we did very little. They took me out to eat for every meal and made sure that I had what I needed. It was a quick trip; they just wanted to make sure that I was okay. Once they saw that I was, they turned around and went home, still worried but cautiously optimistic.

Over the next month, I gradually started to feel like my old self again. I was going to my doctor's appointments every week and even signed myself up for an HIV support group for young men who had been recently diagnosed. Through this group, I met a number of truly loving, gifted, and beautiful young men. Knowing we had something in common allowed us to connect quickly. And while it felt like a negative situation, we would joke all the time in our weekly meetings about keeping it "positive."

I became extremely close with one of the group members, Jay. He was small of size but big on spice, a Cuban American originally from Florida. We were immediately inseparable. More often than not, we would leave the weekly meetings together and head back to his apartment to watch TV and smoke a copious number of blunts. On our days off from work, we would meet up in the Village or on the pier and smoke.

Our routine was fun at first, but the seriousness of my situation was becoming undeniable. Yes, I was feeling physically better, but emotionally and spiritually I was utterly destroyed. Smoking weed with Jay was a little escape from the pain I was facing, but I needed it to be gone completely.

The walls of my world started to compress in the months that followed. The darkness that overtook me ultimately provided the fuel that I would use to stoke a new fire. It would take years to unravel those experiences and transform them into positivity, but redemption was not assured while I was spiraling. During that time in my journey, I quickly lost view of the path of thriving that my parents had hoped for me. My mind—the source of all troubles—convinced me that I was flourishing, when in actuality, with each passing day a portion of my soul evaporated into the drugs I smoked. Chemically induced rose-colored glasses obscured the reality of my fast-devolving situation. I was chasing a high to fill the growing emptiness with anything to feel good, even to feel at all.

■ ■ ■

My mental health was crumbling, and I started to fully give into my addictions once again. I was possessed of an unbelievable desire to have someone take care of me. Naturally, my thoughts drifted to Felik, the present and proximal choice.

One night I started to plan a lie, conspiring to persuade Felik to let me move in with him permanently. I would tell him that eviction notices had been placed on my apartment building's front doors and that the building was being condemned. This wasn't a complete fabrication. My apartment building, a crummy townhouse divided into four apartments, was in deplorable condition and was infested with mice. The owners of the building were months behind on their property taxes, and I wasn't lying that there had been eviction notices; they just hadn't been on my apartment door. He agreed to let me move in with him. The situation would be temporary though, because Felik didn't want a live-in boyfriend; he still wanted to have lots of anonymous sex and meth parties. I also wanted that, so I thought it would be a good fit. However, after a couple contentious months riddled with jealous fights and stolen meth, he kicked me out.

Without Felik's apartment, and without an apartment of my own, I needed to find other accommodation. I bounced around on friends' couches and occasionally got an escorting client who let me stay for the night. Around that time, I came across a client who sparked my interest. He was willing to pay me $3,000 for an entire weekend. I was always open and honest about my HIV status with potential sexual partners. If they were willing, so was I. Here was an opportunity, money, and a place to stay. There was only one catch: he insisted that I be blindfolded the entire time.

The dollar sign spoke louder than the potential fears brewing at the prospect of being blindfolded with a stranger for an entire weekend. Against my better judgment, I wrote down his address and jumped on the next uptown 6 train. When I reached his apartment, a long thick piece of black fabric choked the doorknob and bore a fore-boding note. *Blindfold yourself with this before knocking on the door.* My stomach began to rend. I took a deep breath and focused on the money. I did as the note instructed, knocked on the door, and waited. Footsteps approached. I tried to ward off a premonition of doubt and used my mind's eye to conjure an image of green bills under the black stripe of the blindfold. It was too late. My skin prickled as the door opened and an icy breeze ripped past me. I was pulled inside.

I am not sure how I survived that night. My guardian angels battled shadows on my behalf. While I don't know who they were, they *were* with me, and they were powerful. I was clawed at, rammed down, and tied to the bed, still blindfolded. The evil men that encircled me were many, their guttural utterances an indistinguishable clatter. Perhaps there were six, possibly ten, and their sadistic voices approved from the corners.

The night's lessons came hard. First, choosing to be a sex worker doesn't ensure the sex will always be consensual. More practically, I learned never to blindfold myself before going into a stranger's house. Finally, I learned to get paid upfront. The indignity of not getting paid only added to my anguish at the horrible incident.

My acts of desperation continued even after that night. Once again, I was selling my body for money (getting paid upfront). I made enough to afford a room in Harlem, two blocks away from my first apartment in the city, but I had to move again soon because the building became infested with bedbugs.

I called my friend Kathleen, who lived just a few blocks away, and I explained my desperate housing situation. After speaking with her roommates, she graciously allowed me to stay on their couch. The invitation was open for as long as I needed.

Moving into Kathleen's apartment, which she and her roommates called the Peace Pad, was a safer life. I didn't need to worry about finding enough money to pay exorbitant rent or find a place to sleep. But I took my friends' generosity for granted and didn't even try to contribute. For the first few months, I didn't pay anything, despite getting assistance from the government. That money was going toward my drug use. It wasn't long before it became obvious to Kathleen and her roommates that I was taking advantage of them. I could see that they were getting annoyed, so I started to come home less and less.

By continuing to escort, prostituting myself, I would avoid the problem. Then one night, when I did come home, Kathleen asked to speak with me in her room. She addressed the concerns that the household had. In addition to being concerned that I wasn't paying rent or helping out in any way, they were also worried for my safety. She could see that I was losing a lot of weight, and rapidly.

It had been almost a year since my HIV diagnosis and I was back to my old self-destructive habits, which meant I was constantly forgetting to take my medication. Taking them inconsistently made them less effective, so I was forced to switch medications over and over. Each time I would find myself becoming sicker and sicker. By subconsciously making things more complicated, I could continue to feel sorry for myself, and hope that others would feel sorry for me, allowing me to take advantage of their kindness. The sick cycle continued.

After Kathleen brought it to my attention that I needed to start paying rent, I quickly figured out how to have the government housing assistance pay for a room at the Peace Pad. I was so beholden to the grips of my addiction that, rather than using the government assistance program to enable me to get established in a better situation, I instead used it to get comfortable with not showing up for myself. I continued partying and living in my disturbed fantasies and delusions. I was broken. This new reality I was living was abysmal. I was HIV positive, unbearably depressed, and completely enslaved by the death grip of my addiction to crystal meth.

Dating sites provided easy points of access to crystal meth. I came across a guy on Grindr named Ian who lived down in the West Village on Bank Street. His profile picture was mysterious and visually vague, offering no clue what he looked like, but I didn't care. I was only looking for my next high. Sex was far from the forefront of my mind; only the drugs mattered now.

Ian had said he was alone, but when I arrived, he was anything but. All the main apartment lights were off, with the curtains tightly shut. A venomous neon glow encased the room, emanating from several strategic blacklights. Repellent laughter and deviant voices escaped from the back bedroom.

"I thought you said you were alone," I pointed out with a husk of irritation in my voice.

"I would have said anything to get a piece of that." Ian brushed off my trepidation, grabbing my ass and pulling me close. His forcefulness was a huge turn-on. I quickly forgot about my worry of having other people present. He was a tall man with deathly pale skin and dark circles like the devil's cradle under his eyes. My craving allowed me to look past his ghoulish countenance. As I mentioned, I didn't care if I was with an Adonis or with the creature from the black lagoon, as long as they could get me high. If sex happened afterward, then so be it. And usually that *is* what happened afterward. It was the only way I could pay for the drugs.

It was unsurprising, and much to my delight, when I discovered that Ian's apartment was a drug den, a revolving door of men seeking either sex or their next fix. I was no different, except that while they would leave and return a few days later, I never left after my feet first crossed the threshold.

After talking with Ian on his bed for only a minute, the glass pipe was pulled out fully loaded with crystal. We had wasted no time. I told him that I was HIV positive and wanted to be fully open about my status. He informed me that almost every guy in the apartment was too, and so was he. Nobody there cared, so I didn't either.

I put my lips to the glass pipe. Within seconds, my brain departed my body, and I was sucked in the vacuum abyss of yet another bottomless high. Within 30 minutes, the matter composing my form was passed around to pleasure every man present, while my mind remained disembodied and disassociated far away. This cycle continued throughout the night and for many nights to come, phantasms feasting on my flesh as I writhed in the neon mist of intoxication. The shadowy weeks that followed were among the darkest of my adult life. I was unprepared for how dark they would get. Death loomed from the moment I entered Ian's apartment.

Breathe. When my body is telling me that something is wrong, I will now listen to it. My body is not capable of lying to me.

Breathe. The darkest times in my life have so many windows of hope and opportunity. I will do my best not to be discouraged, for I now know that there will be answers.

Breathe. Sometimes it might feel like I am at the end with no hope in sight. But it is amazing how the will to survive kicks in when I run out of options.

I will breathe and keep moving forward.

---

17 | Hurricane Bruce

> Breathe. No matter how much you love a delusion, it is not real, and it does not love you back.
>
> Breathe. There are many things out of your control. When the hurricane comes, you do have control over seeking shelter or standing in the way of the storm. That choice is yours.
>
> Breathe. Sometimes we need to hit rock bottom, open the trap door, and hit another layer of rock bottom underneath before we decide enough is enough. If you are still alive at your rock bottom, you still have options.
>
> Breathe, and keep moving forward.

For two weeks I hardly left Ian's except to go to the corner store for cigarettes. On these rare outings, Ian would be right by my side. We had fallen for each other. I was obsessed with him, and he was protective, or rather possessive, of me. However, at that time in my life, and under the illusion of the narcotics, I interpreted his behavior as protection.

The routine was always the same. After our brief errands, we would immediately return to the apartment—his sanctum of control—to partake in recurring rendezvous with him and his friends. This lifestyle seemed comfortable to me, as though it were what I deserved. During those weeks, I didn't check in with Kathleen or anyone else from the Peace Pad. This is also one of the many unfortunate gifts that addiction gives its sufferers; you stop communicating with the people you love. I hadn't sent any texts, let alone made a phone call, to let them know that I was at a friend's house, or even alive. I didn't want to go back to the Peace Pad, which felt better than anything I deserved. I also didn't want to go back because I couldn't do drugs or have careless sex with a revolving door of strangers.

But after two weeks, I decided I needed to head back to pack more things for Ian's. I was home at the Peace Pad only one night before returning. While there, I noticed that the energy became thick with tension the instant I walked through the door. With the others present, Kathleen gently asked me where I had been. I gave a truncated answer, stating I had met someone and was staying at their apartment. "You've lost some weight," Kathleen ventured calmly, looking me up and down. I thought I was good at lying but I'm sure she knew, or suspected, what was going on. I tried to sidestep the implications of her observation, instead telling her that I had been eating much healthier and working out more, both complete lies. I was hardly eating at all. I was looking more like Ian with every passing day, becoming skinnier, paler, and developing a dark devil's cradle under my eyes. Even my cheekbones were beginning to stick out a little more. I thought I looked gorgeous.

After Kathleen's gentle, caring interrogation, I collected what I needed and headed back down to Ian's. The merry-go-round of men and drugs continued, every day, and every night. We would stay up into the wee hours getting high, or we would stay up for a few days until we crashed, slept for 14 hours, and repeated the pattern. It was absolute hell and for some reason I loved it. I had been at Ian's for about three months when Hurricane Sandy started to spin our way.

Hurricanes were never a concern while growing up in Montana, and my experience in New York was also limited. I started seeing warnings on the news that the city was shutting down, and so were the subways. This was extremely unusual and immediately sent up a red flag. A small voice of common sense entered my mind. *Maybe I should go back to the Peace Pad and let this storm pass.* Ian agreed with me that I should leave and come back when the worst of the storm was over. He gave me some drugs to last for a few days and sent me on my way.

I made it to the subway station about 30 minutes before they were to shut down, hopped on the uptown A train, and headed home. When I arrived, all my roommates were huddled up in the living room. Big Xs made out of tape crossed the windows to prevent them from shattering. The kitchen counter was lined with water jugs and the cupboards were stocked with food and canned goods that could last us until the end of time.

The Peace Pad was, as always, a very welcoming apartment. Kathleen and her roommates, Adina and Tiffany, let me stay, along with two other young actors, Micah and Caitlyn, who had moved in temporarily with their dog, Wiley. Six people and a dog was simply too many for a Manhattan three-bedroom, one-bath apartment. This was readily apparent as we hunkered down in the living room and waited nervously for Hurricane Sandy to wreak its predicted havoc. We passed the uncertain hours, distracting ourselves with games. As the night grew darker, the wind became louder and stronger. It beat the windows, demanding attention, as the lights did the same, flickering on and off like in a horror movie.

I went to the bathroom to try and calm myself, meth from earlier still swirling in my veins. I thought, incorrectly, that perhaps if I smoked more, it would calm me down and I wouldn't even notice the storm whirling outside. I opened the small bathroom window and blew the smoke outside, where it joined the eddying chaos blowing past. But all I had succeeded in doing was to create a hurricane within my own head. My paranoia spiraled. I went back into the living room, where the games continued. At this point, everyone was a bit loopy because, while I was in the bathroom smoking meth, everyone else was in the living room smoking weed.

The windows had begun to rattle in a disconcerting rhythm, beaten by the force of the wind. As the wind became more intense, so did their shaking. My anxiety increased in kind; I was sure the panes would break at any moment. I had been whipped up into a full panic when I started to repeat vehemently, "Quick, hot glue the windows! Hot glue the windows!" Then my pleadings switched to, "Where is the nearest hospital? If one of us gets hurt, where do we go? I don't know where a hospital is around Harlem. Where is a hospital?" I was so scared that I was shaking, my panic a storm of its own. Kathleen joked, layered with honesty, that dealing with me during the hurricane was worse than the actual hurricane. "You were like Hurricane Bruce. It was almost impossible to calm you down."

My alarm must have spread, because Kathleen decided that we should all leave the living room and hunker in her bedroom. It was the room closest to the center of the building structure. She thought it offered more protection. The other rooms had exterior-facing walls, vulnerable to projectiles and flying glass should the windows indeed break.

We must have been in her room for an hour before I started to breathe at a normal human pace. I joined the others by smoking as much weed as I possibly could, trying to knock myself out. Thankfully, it worked. The six of us, and Wiley, had piled onto Kathleen's full-sized bed, when we realized there was no way we would be able to sleep through the night this way. So some grabbed pillows from the couch and made makeshift beds on the floor. We didn't emerge until morning.

The sun peeked over the prewar buildings, revealing a calm, bright-blue sky. Kathleen, Adina, and Caitlyn went down to the street and took a walk to assess what damage Hurricane Sandy had caused to the neighborhood. We had escaped the worst of its destruction. Harlem had scraped by with a smattering of snapped tree branches and a blanketing of litter in the streets from overturned trash bins. Everywhere except for Upper Manhattan was hit hard. We saw videos of the subways flooding completely, and lower Manhattan was submerged in some places to a height of 8 feet. Power was out everywhere below 14th Street and many of the surrounding boroughs and coastlines were completely wrecked. The basements and first levels of many homes were flooded, destroying everything. In some areas of New Jersey, houses were entirely gone.

Still in a haze and under the grips of my addiction, I couldn't see the folly in heading south. But I was itching to get back to Ian's.

■ ■ ■

Back at Ian's, the apartment was cold. It was below 14th Street, and all the power was out, possibly for days. Nighttime started to rumble in and so did our hunger. The electric stove was useless to us, and takeout wasn't an option since the restaurants were all closed. We decided to warm soup to a bearable temperature by holding it above the flames of our torches, the same ones we used to smoke meth. I remember sitting for close to 30 minutes, turning the cans above the miniature flame, trying my best not to lose patience. The second we saw a single pathetic swirl of steam rise out of the top of the tin, we decided it had been heated enough. I placed a spoonful in my mouth. It was tepid at best, barely more than cool, but I was impatient and didn't want to wait any longer. Besides, we had to be sure not to waste too much of our fuel; we had smoking to get to as soon as we had eaten. Getting high was still my priority. We quickly sucked down the alphabet soup and crawled under the covers to keep warm. Why I chose to leave the safety and warmth of the Peace Pad to come down to an apartment with no electricity during the aftermath of a hurricane still blows my mind. Again, the power of addiction makes us do really stupid things.

The cold and the wet did nothing for my health. After one more week, shivering in the dark and high as a kite, a sickness started to kick in. It was a familiar misery, the kind of sickness that I had felt in the lead-up to my HIV diagnosis. I was unable to leave the bed and every muscle in my body ached in unbearable pain. A few days later, I couldn't even keep down water. Food was impossible. There was no denying my ill condition. I told Ian I needed help getting to my doctor's office. He didn't have a hookup coming or a drug deal to attend to, so I was in luck. If he had, I'm not sure what we would have done. He helped me down the stairs and into the car. I could barely stand.

He dropped me off at the Mount Sinai Clinic on 25th Street, and I hobbled through the lobby and into the elevator, in an astonishing feat of determination. My vision had started to blur, and I had become exceptionally dizzy. After checking in, the nurse came to get me immediately. It was obvious that I was in an extremely poor condition. I waited in an exam room for about 15 minutes before my doctor arrived. He took my vitals and performed a physical examination, then inserted a needle to extract blood to send to the lab for further testing.

"Have you been consistent with taking your medication?" he asked.

"For the most part. Some days I forget," I replied shamefully. Although my doctors frequently asked about my obvious drug use, I always denied it. Since they couldn't help me with my honesty, they kept their attention on my prescription drugs. When I was first diagnosed, I was informed that it was essential I take my medication like clockwork and not miss a dose. Miss too many in a row, and my system could become immune to the medication. I knew better, but when I was with Ian and getting high, I would lose track of time. I didn't know when it was day or when it was night. Time both flew by and inched along. Within the walls of the drug den, the passing of moments blurred into a strange timeless vortex. While I was ceaselessly high, I infinitely hated myself. In that state, I didn't do things that were good for me. Not taking my medicine was just one example. I constantly missed my doses. My HIV viral load—the amount of virus in my bloodstream—was out of control.

In a confusing contradiction of sensations, my temperature was spiking into a fever, even as I was shaking uncontrollably, feeling like I might turn to ice. In less than 10 minutes I was loaded into the back of an ambulance and dashed to the hospital's Upper East Side location. One of my most crystal-clear memories from that traumatic day happened as I was laying on the gurney being wheeled across the busy sidewalk just outside the building. A person passed by with pity in their eyes and, sensing probable death, said, "Hang in there, buddy. You are going to be okay." It was then I lost consciousness.

I woke up in the emergency room with an IV in my arm and a monitor on my chest and finger. Not only was my HIV viral load out of control, but I had acquired acute hepatitis C and pneumonia. My skin was yellow, my urine was brown, and I had uncontrollable diarrhea. I was dying. Once a bed opened up, I was moved into a room and placed under quarantine. This is where I would stay for the next 10 days.

During my stay, I became broken. It was akin to the feeling I had in Las Vegas when I was 16. *Do or die.*

I couldn't die. Despite all the self-hatred, I still had a light inside of me that wanted to live, that wanted to shine. I felt deep in my heart that I still had dreams to accomplish. At the same time, I felt trapped, like I would never get out of the hell I was in. Over the next 10 days, I had the distance, the solitude, and the time to think. I also had enough time to detox from the drugs that were altering my mind and obscuring my vision of the way back to the old familiar path.

I called Kathleen and let her know where I was and that I was truly so sorry for everything. Being honest to even one person was a start. Once my quarantine was lifted and I was becoming more stable, Kathleen came to visit me. She walked into the room wearing a protective hospital gown and a white net cap on her head. Even though my quarantine was lifted, the medical staff were still making everyone take precautions for their own safety. She greeted me with the warmest smile and a mason jar of sunflowers. She also brought me a collection of magazines to flip through to help pass the time. She kept me company, chatting from the corner chair. I was still very weak so she didn't stay long, but she made sure I knew that I was loved. I hope that I have returned the kind gesture to her in the years since; I am sure I did not in that moment.

Eventually I started to feel better and much more stable. The doctors had put me on new HIV medication that was hopefully starting to do its job. The unendurable physical pain had finally dissipated, and all the boxes seemed to check off for my adequate health, so I was discharged, this time with pamphlets about acute hepatitis C.

I had squeaked by. But lessons are easily forgotten, and addictions are powerful. The second I left the hospital, I turned left to cross the street and walked directly into a corner bodega to buy a pack of cigarettes. I was looking for a fix, any fix. I smoked three in quick succession, then hopped in a cab and headed home to the Peace Pad. In the cab, I readjusted. I had gone 10 days without cigarettes. This wasn't how I wanted to move forward. When I got back to the apartment, I went straight into the bathroom and rammed the pack of cigarettes under the faucet, soaking them in water before chucking them in the trash can.

The experience I had just gone through should have been enough to keep me safe, sane, and sober moving forward. But the only thing I wanted to do was go back to Ian's and get high. I waited a few more days before I gave in. It was true: in my mind, in my compulsions, in my addictions, I was Hurricane Bruce.

It took no time to slip back into the abyss of my addictions and the uncomfortable darkness of Ian's home. Shortly after I returned, we were invited to a party at a gay hotel in Hell's Kitchen. Without hesitating, we went. There were five other men in the hotel room when we arrived. Porn was already playing on the TV and the smell of meth flooded the room. I jumped in the shower to prepare myself for the orgy I anticipated. To my disappointment, when I got out of the shower, I found that sex was not on the table. They just wanted to hang out, watch porn together, and smoke meth. No sex? This was not really what I was looking for. Getting high was these guys' only objective. Once I was high enough, I decided to leave.

In a daze, I went for a long walk. I left Hell's Kitchen, headed south, and ended up in Chelsea. I stumbled on a high-end thrift store where Prada, Gucci, Louis Vuitton, Dolce and Gabbana, and a mix of other luxury brands lined the walls.

A pair of black Prada pants caught my eye. As I walked into the dressing room, I saw some hangers that were left on a hook. Then the thought hit me. *I could steal these pants.* I had zero intention of stealing anything when I walked into the shop, but the empty hangers triggered something in me. I tried on the pants, and they fit me like a glove. The pants I was wearing when I walked in would easily slide right over the skin-tight Prada pair.

I pulled my own pants over the coveted item, and then stepped out of the dressing room and handed back the remaining items, pretending I didn't want anything. My mistake: I also handed back an empty hanger.

"Do you have the pants with you?" the store clerk asked.

"I didn't try them on. I thought I gave those back to you?" I replied foolishly.

"You took them into the dressing room, and we will need those back," she insisted sharply.

I became defensive and doubled down with my excuses. "How dare you accuse me of stealing!" I began to panic and looked for an opportunity to bolt out of the front door. *Now!* I reached over the counter and grabbed my checked bag. Like lightning, I ran toward the front door. The store owner jumped in my way. I wasn't going to let a gray-haired woman in her 50s stop me. My heart was racing at a hundred miles per hour. I tackled her through the front door, causing us both to fall onto the sidewalk in front of the shop. The other store clerk then jumped on top of me, pinning me to the ground. Arms and legs flailed as I kicked and pushed, trying to break free from their hold.

A man passing by saw our struggle and heard the store owner's cries. "Help! Stop him, he stole from my shop!" He added to the pile, jumping on top of me as well, to help pin me down. I gave in. Laying there on my back with the store clerk and this strange man on top of me, I stared up to the sky. The fog of my high ended abruptly, though temporarily. For a stark moment I was painfully lucid. I began to cry. I was scared, embarrassed, ashamed.

The clerk's knee had moved to my chest. She began to scream at me. "I know you think you are tough shit, but you are not. Look at yourself, kid—you are not very cute! You are going to jail!" She repeated again and again, "You are *not* cute! You are *not* cute!"

Moments later the police arrived and took over. I was handcuffed and taken to the squad car. They hadn't yet searched my bag, but I knew they would. I looked at the female officer and truthfully and straight-forwardly told her, "I have drugs on me."

She looked at me in surprise. "You do? What kind?" I informed her that I had meth and a pipe to go with it in the sunglasses case. "Good for you for being honest, that will help in your case," she replied. I felt that she had seen me in that moment for what I was, a struggling human being, rather than a criminal.

This was my first time being arrested as an adult and I was absolutely terrified. There was no escaping my appearance. I was going to stand out like a sore thumb in jail. My androgynous black pants and mesh vest shirt that had ripped in the struggle were a calling card, invit-ing unwanted trouble. I sat alone in a cell for 10 hours before being moved to the jail downtown, where there was a depressingly long line of men waiting to be incarcerated. I was one of them.

I was led to a huge tomblike room with massive cells on either side. There were probably four of these cells per side with about 20 to 50 people in each cell. The harsh industrial light bounced off the blue surfaces, transforming the shade and suffusing everything with an unappealing green pallor. The many metal bars created a black striped pattern and divided my view of the souls and shadows pacing behind them. There was one lonely stainless-steel toilet and sink up on a platform in the corner of the cell I was placed in. It was com-pletely visible to everyone around. *Like hell am I going to be using that,* I thought to myself.

Stay awake, keep going, stay awake, keep going, I chanted to myself, scared shitless to fall asleep in the mix of all these other desperate and poten-tially violent men. After probably three hours of sitting on my hands, rocking back and forth and chanting *stay awake, keep going, stay awake, keep going,* I was transported to another cell closer to the court room.

This was a much smaller cell that had about 15 people in it. I sat again on a long cinder-block bench and continued to rock back and forth chanting *stay awake, keep going, stay awake, keep going*. I started to crash as my high wore off. I had been locked up for nearly 20 hours when, unexpectedly, I was shaken awake by one of the other inmates.

"Dude, I thought you were dead. I've been shaking you for like 10 minutes," he said. "The public defender is here and wants to speak with you."

Fighting an intense lingering drowsiness, I found my footing and walked into a closet-like cinder-block room that had a metal stool screwed to the floor. A glass window divided the space in front of me. I felt half asleep. My lawyer was a blonde woman who waited patiently for me to wake up. Once I was a little more coherent, we began going over my case

One hour later I was standing in front of the judge and listening to my charge. Because it was my first offense, I was let go with a follow-up court date. I took my paperwork and walked out of the courthouse with a MetroCard in hand. It was preloaded with two rides so that I could get to the police precinct, where I had been the day before, to retrieve my bag, which they had kept. After that awkward task, I headed straight home to the Peace Pad, back toward the familiar path. When I got home, Kathleen was sitting on the couch watching TV. "What the hell happened to you?" she asked noticing my ripped mesh vest and bedraggled appearance. I looked like shit.

"I was arrested for jumping the turnstile on the subway," I lied, not ready to be fully truthful and unable to handle interactions with others. Her positivity and kindness couldn't yet be received. I walked straight past her into my room, where I threw myself onto the air mattress and slept for many hours.

At some point the next day, I awoke. I was completely sick of myself and the hurricane I was living. I wanted to be free from this hell that ensnared me.

I didn't need to be ready. I simply needed to be willing. And I was willing. With this gift of desperation, I got onto my computer and started looking for addiction resources within the city. To my surprise, many different programs popped up: inpatient and outpatient rehabs as well as 12-step meetings. Then I came across one tab that read, "The Addiction Institute of New York." I clicked on it and called the number provided. This was *the* phone call that would change my life for the better.

I scheduled an evaluation appointment for the next day. I followed through with it, and actually showed up early. The Addiction Institute was going to be the place that would change my life forever.

Breathe. No matter how much I love a delusion, it is not real and it does not love me back.

Breathe. There are many things out of my control. But when the hurricane comes, I do have control over seeking shelter or standing in the path of the storm. That choice is mine.

Breathe. Sometimes I need to hit rock bottom, open the trap door, and hit another layer of rock bottom underneath before I decide enough is enough. If I am still alive at rock bottom, I now know that I still have options.

I will breathe and keep moving forward.

18

Crystal in the Rain

Breathe. There is help out there for exactly what you are dealing with. You don't have to be ready, you just have to be willing to receive it.

Breathe. If you think you are taking the easier or softer way out, think again. Anything worthwhile takes a lot of hard work, but that hard work will pay off.

Breathe. When you finally get out of your own way, you will find that you are ready to receive everything you have ever wanted.

Breathe and keep moving forward.

My treatment plan at the Addiction Institute of New York was to be placed in the outpatient rehab program. I would attend several different meetings, four days a week, as well as have an individual therapy session.

Some of the meetings were DBT (dialectical behavioral therapy) and CBT (cognitive behavioral therapy), which I was unfamiliar with.

The leaders explained that DBT is a form of talk therapy. It allows people who feel intense emotions to find a place of peace by helping them understand and accept difficult feelings. CBT focuses on current problems. It helps people recognize destructive behaviors and offers them better techniques for handling these situations. *Yes, that sounds like something I need.*

I also attended meetings for people with addictions and sessions about harm reduction, which is intended to decrease the negative consequences of risky drug and sexual activity when complete abstinence is not desired. It allows people to make positive changes to help protect themselves and others while still engaging in harmful behaviors. I learned that it is important to be very careful with this approach, and that people should understand what they hope to get from going down that road. This includes asking yourself whether you really want a positive change, or whether you are using harm reduction as an excuse to enable yourself to continue using your drug of choice. Is harm reduction an excuse to transfer your addiction to another harmful habit that you judge to be less bad? Ultimately, this style of recovery was not for me. I wanted to be sober.

Finally, my outpatient rehab included Crystal Meth Anonymous for Gay Men, which was especially triggering for me because I was around gay men who were still using. My first though was *What an amazing way to hook up and find my next fix*, and this did happen a few times. Although the group was specifically oriented to help people like me who used meth, I quickly realized that it was not safe for my recovery.

Even after being arrested and having my health deteriorate, I wasn't motivated to quit cold turkey. Late at night, I would find myself getting online, searching for my next fix. This habit continued for two months, even while I was participating in the outpatient program. In spite of my relapses, I continued to go to my scheduled meetings and was open and honest that I was still struggling and using, and the more I attended the outpatient program, the more my drug intake declined. This progress was enough to sustain me. *I think I can quit, I can keep moving forward, I think I can quit, I can keep moving forward.*

When an online search had led me to the Addiction Institute of New York, I had shown my willingness to give up drugs, but I wasn't ready to fully commit to the program and follow through until months later. *You don't have to be ready; you just have to be willing. Eventually, the readiness will come.*

One night I had smoked a small amount of meth with a stranger in a hotel in Hell's Kitchen, despite not wanting to. There was nothing positive or enjoyable about the experience. After taking two hits I became very nauseous and my head began to pound violently. I was hugging the toilet for the remainder of the night. The pounding made me feel as if my brain was melting out of my ears. It was horrible. I was tired of doing this to myself. I felt helpless and broken and completely defeated.

After a turbulent taxi ride home, I went to bed and sobered up. The next morning, something had changed. I saw the ugly and the good. I saw the welts on my skin, the caves under my eyes, the scratches across my face, the weight I had lost, and the deadness in my eyes. There was something beautiful here, though. The gift of desperation outshined the darkness and allowed me to see something I hadn't seen before. I was able to truly see myself for the first time. I could see my own potential to be better and allowed the light of recognition to expand.

The addiction had pushed my capability to do more into the shadows, unseen. As the morning light of awareness broke in, I started to see the soft glowing outline of my desire to do something positive with my days, of my capacity for empathy and compassion. From the outside, nothing was happening, but my internal scales were tipping.

I had connected to my worth, my potential, my desire to live, and my desire to give. Since I was alive, I chose to embrace it.

By changing the direction of my attention, I found the power of perception and acknowledged my own worth. I was capable of so much good, in spite of all the bad.

I was ready. I could no longer approach recovery half-heartedly.

There was a mausoleum cemetery not too far from the Peace Pad, in the Sugar Hill neighborhood of Harlem. I felt inexplicably called to visit it. I grabbed my meth pipe as well as anything that had to do with my drug use and put it in a bag. Desperate to destroy the addiction that was stealing my life, I headed off to the cemetery, committed and ready.

As I slowly passed through the gates, I took in the full bloom of the trees that towered over me. Still feeling the effects from the night before, I dragged my feet down the pathway. It led to a small hilltop created by granite mausoleums whose entrances extended into the earth behind and over the top. I continued up the hill and found a grassy area to sit just above the mausoleum facades. As I sat down, I began to speak to the universe, offering my full confession. I begged the higher powers-that-be to remove the demon of addiction that had its grip on me. Not knowing to whom or to what I was praying, I had no other choice but to surrender. I prayed in earnest sincerity for 30 minutes to a power outside of and greater than myself. Then I found a smooth, round rock on the ground. I reached inside my bag and pulled out the crystal meth, pipe, and torch, and placed it on the ground in front of me. With passion, anguish, and sadness I grabbed the rock and began to crush the crystals and pipe, turning them into meaningless dust. After obliterating these tools of demise, I pushed the remains into the vent of a mausoleum, glass shards, crystal dust, and all. The instant I did so, like a cleansing acknowledgment from the heavens, it began to rain. A crushing burden had been lifted. I had been shackled to my addiction before birth, but now I felt truly free. In the gentle falling rain, I started to cry great heaping sobs of relief. It was as though the rain was dissolving the nightmare world I had been living in.

The shower was short, and I sat on the hill in the cemetery until it stopped. The sun peeked brightly from behind a dark cloud, announcing even more light to come. The storm clouds kept moving forward, allowing the sun to reveal its full glory. I took this as a sign. *So must I.* The authentic me was starting to pierce through for the first time in years.

June 13, 2014, was the date that set me fully free. I released myself from the shackles with the mirror-key that was myself and my potential. I was positive that I could find the "old familiar path," even when my view might be obscured by gloom and negativity in the future. The way forward could be found with recognition and willingness.

For the remainder of the day, I sat in the living room of the Peace Pad watching crap TV and figuratively licking my wounds. As nighttime came, I headed to bed and fell peacefully asleep.

I began to dream. My peace had another survival battle yet to fight. As I descended into unconsciousness, I found myself standing in the nightmare that had haunted me before.

The villainous shadow lurched out of the green-and-black-striped walls and landed within a hair's breadth of me. It unfolded from its crouched position and explored the space around me in a methodical feline manner. When it was directly in front of me, it straightened up to the full 13 feet of its form. Its hideous waist exposed decades of starvation.

Its arm jetted out to the side in an angular manner, gripping the familiar syringe. Its tip was just as menacing as before, long, thin, and awaiting its orders. An unseen force seized my legs, waist, and arms, instantly strapping them to the dreaded metal chair.

The black stripes along the wall turned to mirrors, revealing my reflection in a kaleidoscopic fractal. I knew I was in danger.

The floor to my left began to shake and a trap door vomited forth a cart with three labeled boxes. The first box was scrawled with "HIV," the second was labeled "Weakness," and the final box bore the four-letter inscription "Meth." In my previous visits to this phantom torture chamber, the boxes had been labeled "Brain," "Heart," and "Voice Box." My organs had been stolen, but this time I remained intact. My brain was forming thoughts, my heart was pounding a million miles an hour, and I suddenly heard myself screaming. In that moment, I was no longer this monster's marionette.

The silhouette moved closer. I could smell its rotting skin as it bellowed toward me. "Do you know what is in this syringe?" it asked as a subtle smirk crept across its face.

Again, I shook my head no.

It laughed in demonic amusement. "Of course you don't! It's always more fun to find out what it is after it's already been forced inside you!" The shadow's voice seethed with bitterness. Its eyes darted from the tip of the needle to my unprotected arm, then directly into my eyes faster than I could blink.

It slowly raised the needle into the air over my vulnerable flesh, then let out a frustrated, high-pitched scream as it slammed the glass syringe to the floor, where it shattered into thousands of pieces.

With an expression of unvarnished anger, it reached for the cart, ripping open the three boxes to reveal a single syringe within each. One by one the dark entity grabbed them, ferociously raising them high above me, and striving to inject their poison into my arms. His fury was futile. With each attempt, his malicious motions were deflected by some unseen force. The syringes slammed to the ground, shattering on impact into a crystal pattern of shards. His frustrated shrieks fell mute. As the final syringe shattered, so did the monstrous shadow, vanishing in the black dust of an ash cloud.

I jolted up out of my sleep, sweating and shaking. The meaning of my dream was crystal clear. I had finally freed myself from the death grip of my addiction to meth, sex, and self-hatred. My heart rate slowed to a normal pace. I sat in the silence in my room, noticing the peace and serenity. I began to take very deep breaths and my heart rate slowed to a normal pace. *I am okay. I am safe. I will keep moving forward. Just keep breathing.*

■　■　■

I continued my treatment at the Addiction Institute for a year and a half before graduating out of the program. During that time, I was able to find self-love and joy. I was also able to find a job and keep it. I started to regain the trust of my friends and family, and life was coming back slowly and surely with every passing day. Finally, the simple joy of living was back in my day-to-day routine.

It wasn't without great struggle. I still fought cravings for many months, even after graduating from outpatient rehab, and I still do. However, I now possess the desire and drive to push through those cravings. Very slowly, I learned how to overcome my ego and my fear of asking for help from my friends, family, and even my therapists. I continue going to 12-step meetings, which has helped me immensely.

After going down such a self-destructive road for so long, I had finally made my U-turn. Making my way back to the old familiar path, I had to tackle obstacles head on, but I had seen them before on my downward spiral. Knowing where the pitfalls were, I could navigate through them and avoid potential collisions. The metaphor of climbing uphill is accurate. There is a reason it is employed by so many when documenting their recovery. However, knowing the challenges to come, I was able to face them fully.

Just as with the very beginning of my journey, the odds of recovery were stacked against me, but I have the will to survive. Driven by that will, I continue to keep moving forward. There is much more to my story, and I hope one day to share that with you in future books. In this memoir, and in my daily postings on social media, I have shared my shadow work publicly in the conviction that pieces of my journey will be helpful, inspiring, and possibly provide a little bit of hope for you or your loved ones as you keep moving forward. For when we keep moving forward, we will find that there is truly so much good coming our way. The best days of our lives haven't even happened yet. The unfolding horizon holds our hope for all the good to come. I now know this to be true because I never gave up. Since descending into the pits of my hell, I have soared through many hoops. Yes, some of them may have been on fire but still I soared through. Going from being strung out on drugs to sobering up, to owning successful businesses, creating laughter-filled homes, and even writing this book, I'm living proof that anything is possible and we do recover.

Breathe. There is help out there for exactly what I am dealing with. I don't have to be ready, I just have to be willing to receive it.

Breathe. If I think I am taking the easier or softer way out, I will think again. Anything worthwhile takes a lot of hard work, but I know that hard work will pay off.

Breathe. When I finally get out of my own way, I will find that I am ready to receive everything I have ever wanted.

I will breathe and keep moving forward.

Because I can and because I am worth it.

19 | Photo Gallery

Family portrait, 1991: April, Sonia, Megan, and Bruce (left to right)

First day of school: Megan, Bruce, April, and Sonia (left to right)

With permission from Christine

Dusk on the Beaverhead. Glen & Bruce '94

Dusk on the Beaverhead, 1994: Glenn and Bruce

With permission from Charles Lindsay

Adoption day, 1997: Sonia, Glenn, Bruce, Christine, Megan, and April (left to right)

Photo by family friend

Barbie Girl at the family reunion: Bruce and Glenn

With permission from Christine

We heard you! April, Sonia, Christine, Bruce, Glenn, and Megan (left to right)

Photo by family friend

Bruce "playing" guitar
With permission from Sonia

Bruce on break at the candy store in Virginia City, 2006
With permission from Christine

Runaway Bruce, 2007

With permission from Christine

High school graduation, 2009: "I actually did it!"

With permission from Sonia

"Yikes," 2014: Self-portrait in the mirror at the height of my meth addiction.

Bruce Brackett (Author)

Christmas in New York City, 2015: Jay, Kathleen, and Bruce on the subway

Bruce Brackett (Author)

Sheridan, Montana, 2020: Bruce revisiting the house that the siblings lived in with Berna

With permission from Teo

Cheer Choice Awards, Las Vegas, 2023: Bruce and Kathleen

With permission from Teo

Epilogue

"You are breathing very rare air right now." Those are the words that Shannon, from the Wiley publishing team, emailed to me just moments after I completed my first draft. I was indeed breathing rare air, just as I was when my father and I reached the summit of Old Baldy on my first mountain climb.

We—you and I— were connected even then, in that rare air. By reading this, you have accompanied me back to that time and place. Everything that happened since then has led me to the place where I could write these words as an offering of hope and inspiration.

That moment on the mountain is alive even now, and that rare air is available to you, to make a change for yourself, to learn from my experiences, to avoid my heartbreaks, or more simply to know that someone else has been wherever you are. Whatever your challenge, someone has faced it and felt what you are feeling. They, too, felt lost, alone, or less-than. I know I did. When we left our names at the top of Old Baldy, we left behind something of ourselves for future climbers. All of us who share life's mountains leave something behind, even if the light and leaves look different now. Our names, those that have come before, are written down nearby. Even people who reach the summit in solitude are not alone.

It is in that spirit that I have been willing to do this shadow work, to bring it into the light. No one should ever feel alone. Whatever your struggles, someone else has felt that pain. When you feel there is no one else, I am here. I see you. Having been through the darkness, I see you—and you are not alone.

The following is a transcript of what I shared with those of you who were online at the exact moment when I read Shannon's words. My feelings and thoughts in that moment provide an honest summary of why I wrote this memoir and what my hope is for you, for having taken this journey with me.

Huge shimmies!

Holy Jeeps!

I AM breathing really rare air right now. And I am only able to breathe that air because I am sober. I wouldn't be able to have accomplished this drunk. I wouldn't have been able to accomplish this stoned out of my mind, like I was for so many years. I wouldn't have been able to accomplish this high on meth, like I was for so many years. I wouldn't have been able to accomplish this in my self-doubt, or my self-loathing, or my self-hatred that I allowed my mental health to take me into . . . those dark places and dark corners. If I didn't ask for help, if I didn't get back on my bipolar medication, if I wasn't forced into positions that were going to push me in directions to get back on my bipolar medication. Sometimes we have to fall, in order for us to skyrocket.

So maybe take that leap of faith.

And maybe fall a little bit.

And with all of your might, spread your wings . . . and catch some air.

And see . . . what IF you fly.

You can.

The only one who's telling you that you can't is you.

Truly, when we sit down, when we lay down at the end of the day and pull the covers up over our heads, the only one stopping you is you. It doesn't matter what all of these other naysayers have to say. It doesn't matter how many times someone said you weren't good enough, or that you can't accomplish this, or you'll never be able to finish this. The only person allowing those voices to get into your head, to allow you to stop, is you.

And I did that for so many years. I listened to all of the other bullshit that came my way instead of listening to MY truth . . . listening to what I wanted to do. And once I started doing that, my life blossomed . . . in ways I still can't even begin to express, or understand, or fathom. But I don't need to understand it. I just need to accept my current situation . . . no matter what it is. And if I'm able to do that, I can face it. And if I can face it, I can deal with it. And if I can deal with it, I can keep moving forward.

It's not a race. It's not about the accomplishments. It's not about how many times you've fallen. Hell, it's not even about how many times you've gotten back up. It's WHY you get back up. And how you keep moving forward. And WHY you keep moving forward.

(continued)

(continued)

All of the failures are a success.

That shows that you tried . . . that's a success!

Who cares if you failed? So what?!

The only way to know if you're gonna fly is to jump. You gotta take that chance.

So, thank you for your love. Thank you for your encouragement. I send it all right back to you. Every single day that I post [an inspiration video on my social media platforms], I want you to know how much I love you, and how much you inspire me, and how proud I am of you. I know that so many of you go through a day without hearing that. Maybe you go through more days than one, without even hearing that. And I want you to know that I am here . . . in your corner . . . fighting with you . . . and for you. And I will be your cheerleader, in the corner, giving you the biggest shimmies, to let you know that you CAN overcome whatever you are facing.

'Cause if I can do it, despite all of the odds that were stacked against me, YOU can do it too.

You can.

And you're worth it.

Be your own advocate. Even if no one else is advocating for you. Be your own advocate and you will be amazed at what happens.

Dwell in the power of positivity. Your life will transform. It may not happen in a year, it may not happen in 10. This book took me 14 years to accomplish. I started using drugs when I was 16 years old. I am 32 [and in my ninth year of being sober from all hard-core drugs. And it wasn't supposed to happen until I was willing to be ready to rigorously start my journey in sobriety. Recovery is not linear. It doesn't matter when you start your journey. What matters is THAT you start your journey when YOU are willing to be ready]. And I do not "got" this. I will be battling this every single day. The second I think, "Oh, I got this, I can control this". . . I know I am headed for a downward spiral. I know I am headed for a relapse. So to say I am never going to relapse again is very naïve. It actually could happen. Do I want it to happen . . . no. Am I manifesting it to happen . . . absolutely not. Am I scared that it's going to happen . . . yes. And I keep that close to me.

So don't compare yourself to anyone else's journey. Like I always say, when you compare yourself to others, you become bitter. When you compare yourself to yourself, you become better . . . in YOUR time. When YOU are ready. Not when they say you're ready. Not when they say jump. Not when they say do this. When YOU are ready.

You can, and you will.

I love you. Thank you for your love. You are amazing. You are incredible. Don't let anyone tell you differently. If they are telling you differently, they don't need to be in your life.

Thank you for being here.

Give yourself a lot of grace; you've already overcome all the other bullshit in your life to get to this moment, right now.

(*continued*)

(continued)

You can overcome this too. I promise you that. If you've already overcome everything else in your life, what is there to say you can't overcome this too? Get rid of that negative thinking.

Negativity be gone.

Dwell in the power of possibility.

Do your best. Do no harm. And do for yourself every single day, so that you too can eventually do for others. If you can't do for others right now, it just means that you need to be doing for yourself. . . . And that is okay.

I love you.

Whatever it is, you are not alone. Someone else has been there, and we are connected.

Thank you for being here with me.

Resource Guide
for Help Hotlines

United States

Medical Emergency: 911

Mental Emergency: 988 or text 741-741

National Suicide Prevention: 1-800-273-8255

National Domestic Violence: 1-800-799-7233

Family Violence: 1-800-996-6228

Self-Harm Prevention: 1-800-366-8288

American Association of Poison Control Centers: 1-800-222-1222

Substance Abuse and Mental Health Services Administration: 1-800-662-4357

Alcoholism and Drug Dependency: 1-800-622-2255

National Crisis Line, Anorexia and Bulimia: 1-800-233-4357

Lifeline Crisis Chat: contact-usa.org

Veterans Crisis Line: veteranscrisisline.net

Suicide Prevention Wiki: suicideprevention.wikia.com

Alcoholics Anonymous: www.aa.org

Narcotics Anonymous: www.na.org

Canada
Emergency: 911
Crisis Hotline: 1–888–353–2273
Your Life Counts: yourlifecounts.org
Suicide Prevention Wiki: suicideprevention.wikia.com

United Kingdom and Ireland
Emergency: 999 or 112
Hotline (UK, Local Rate): 44 (0) 8457 90 90 90
Hotline (UK, Minicom): 44 (0) 8457 90 91 92
Hotline (ROI, Local Rate): 1850 60 90 90
Hotline (ROI, Minicom): 1850 60 90 91
Suicidal Thoughts and Prevention (UK): nhs.uk
Your Life Counts (UK and Ireland): yourlifecounts.org
Samaritans (UK and Ireland): samaritans.org

Australia
Emergency: 000
Lifeline Australia: 1 300 13 11 14
Your Life Counts: yourlifecounts.org

New Zealand
Emergency: 111
Lifeline 24/7: 0800 543 354
Your Life Counts: yourlifecounts.org

Brazil
Emergency: 190
Life Appreciation Center (Centro de Valorização da Vida): 188, cvv.org.br
Alcoholics Anonymous (A JUNAAB Alcoólicos Anônimos do Brasil): 55–11–3315–9333, aa.org.br
Narcotics Anonymous (Linha de Ajuda Narcóticos Anônimos): 132, na.org.br

Mexico

Safety Hotline: 55 5533-5533, consejociudadanomx.org

Worldwide

Your Life Counts: yourlifecounts.org

Suicide Prevention: befrienders.org

Acknowledgments

This book has been a dream of mine since I was 18 years old. The journey from writing the first words of this book to having it published took me 14 years. It truly took a village to see this book into reality. I would like to give a special thanks to everyone involved in the completion of this dream.

Thank you to Jeannene, Christina, Michelle, Shannon, Michael, Casper, Jozette, Trinity, Amy, and all the team members at Wiley for your love, professional support, and guidance in helping to make this book a physical reality.

I would also like to send a special thank you to my mom, dad, and sisters for always being my number-one supporters. It is your love, belief in me, and support that helps me to keep moving forward and to do the "next right thing."

I would like to thank my friends, and many therapists, social workers, case workers, doctors and psychiatrists, and my sponsor for never giving up on me and for continuing to motivate me in this world that is just oh so wild. You know who you are.

To my online FAN-mily, a special thank you for all of your continued love, support, and encouragement. You are a major reason this book came to be and for its success. You know who you are and you are priceless to me.

Finally, I would like to thank the love of my life, Teo. You know what you do and you know just how much you mean to me. Words could never express my love and gratitude for you. You are my rock and you are my life. Thank you for always being by my side through my ups and downs. I truly hope I return to you what you have so generously given to me.

About the Author

Bruce W. Brackett (BWB) is a social media personality, author, entrepreneur, self-taught visual artist, and international motivational speaker. Originally from southwest Montana, BWB moved to NYC at the age of 18 to pursue his dreams of being on Broadway. After many distractions, making it to Off-Broadway, and developing several addictions, meth being a big one, BWB found his true calling and his way back to sobriety through art and by advocating for recovery to his online audience of over 1.2 million people. This online community of recovery fuels BWB's love, passion, creativity, and mission to share positivity and the possibilities of recovery.

Bruce has sold his artwork and "Negativity Be Gone" hand fans to people in all 50 of the United States and in over 14 countries. BWB now resides with his partner, Teo, and his tuxedo cat, DionE, in the Pocono Mountains, where they enjoy hiking, kayaking, and finding all the beautiful waterfalls.

You may order custom artwork from BWB through his website, bwbart.com, or via his business email, bwbartist@gmail.com.

You may also book Bruce as a keynote speaker for your event or organization though his speaking business email, bwbspeaks@gmail.com.

Index